Ruth Elisabeth
Hancock

WORK
YOUR
Energy

The entrepreneur's guide
to raising your vibration,
tapping into higher consciousness
and achieving more happiness,
wealth and success

R^ethink

First published in Great Britain in 2022 by Rethink Press
(www.rethinkpress.com)

Disclaimer
The advice in this book should not replace proper medical advice from your doctor. It should not serve as medical advice or any form of medical treatment. Please always speak to your doctor before changing any of your medical treatments. This book has been written and published for informational and educational purposes only, so please use it as informational only and not as a substitute for individual or medical care.

Dedicated to my mother

*Wake up to the immense power you have
inside yourself and use it to create the life
and business that your heart wants.*

*Believe that you can and you will, because belief is
everything, and the truth of who you are will set you free.*

Contents

My Story

I started writing this book three years ago, although my story starts much earlier than that. I began writing because I knew I had something to say, but didn't know quite what. It started out as a business book for female entrepreneurs. I never thought I would get so passionate about energy, consciousness and the potential of the energy field, but I did, and with each step I took I got closer to the real me. The energetic me. I knew something had transformed my life, but couldn't quite articulate it. In order to try and understand what had happened, I began to research it.

This book is probably the story of my life, or at the very least, the story of my spiritual awakening. Bizarrely enough, mine came via science rather than spirit. Researchers, scientists and writers like Dr Joe Dispenza,

Dr Bruce Lipton, Nassim Haramein, Lynne McTaggart, Gregg Braden, Ervin Laszlo, Dr David Hawkins, Nikola Tesla, Albert Einstein and many more inspired me. Not only are they innovative thinkers, but they changed the world and stuck fast to their paths, even if they were rocky ones. Their research allowed me to make sense of my life and discover who I really am. Who we all really are.

During my research, I began to suspect that what we refer to as 'phenomena' is actually an energy field, or forces, at work. We have all had personal experiences that we can't make sense of or articulate. *Work Your Energy* is where I share mine as I explore the science behind it. I love magic as much as the next person, but when I realised that magic is real, life definitely got more interesting.

When I discovered that I was made of energy, my thoughts and feelings were made of energy and everything is about 'vibration and wave frequency' or resonance – including me – it transformed my life. You see, the reality of my life was not one that I wanted. I wasn't happy, and I certainly wasn't achieving my dreams, but working harder just wasn't getting me there. When I finally gave up focusing on the external world and began to change my life from the inside out, not only did my life and business shift faster than I could have ever thought possible, but it also came with a whole host of other benefits.

Before I share my 'energetic' secrets of success, let's start with where I was several years ago, because that's where it all began. Two months before our second child was born, my mother-in-law died. My husband applied for a job overseas to escape the pain of losing her. Four months after we arrived, my own mother died back home. With a baby and toddler, a limited support system, no family and a husband working long hours, it wasn't long before I started to crack. I didn't know that at the time, though; I just thought I needed to get back to work.

At first it felt good to be working again. I threw myself back into my career and enjoyed the teamwork, data analysing and report writing, but without proper child-care, trying to juggle home-life and working definitely didn't work for me. After completing three consulting projects while my husband and I juggled time off, I decided to go back to the drawing board on my career.

I thought long and hard about where I could provide the most value with my background and experience and eventually decided to apply my big business knowledge to the small business world by becoming a business coach. I had worked with small to medium-sized enterprises and entrepreneurs before. I found the fast-paced environment challenging and stimulating and also enjoyed working one-on-one with business owners. Helping them find clarity, get the most out of themselves and their teams and strategically grow their businesses allowed me to successfully incorporate my sales and marketing and organisational development background, innate strategic thinking and commercial know-how.

Unfortunately, underneath it all, I was still struggling. I learned the hard way that prioritising your happiness, taking good care of yourself and enjoying what you do is key, but there is so much more to a thriving business – and life – than this.

The grief of losing both mothers at a time when I needed them most, combined with the chaos of trying to bring up small children in an unfamiliar country while my husband was hardly ever at home took its toll. I struggled to keep up with it all. I felt a desperate need to achieve my dreams and could feel the clock ticking on my life, so I pushed myself to work even harder, often working late so I could fit more in when the children were asleep. I threw myself into my business and the resentment towards the rest of my life got me well and truly stuck in the negative. Finally, I couldn't take any more and decided to tackle it.

I didn't know where to start. I just knew I wanted to feel happy again, so I started there. I took some time out to think about when I had last felt happy. As much as my husband and I were arguing in our current circumstances, the happiest day of my life was still my wedding day. I began to think about this and other happy memories. It wasn't the memories I was trying to access – it was the feelings they provoked. I got married late in life, so in addition to happiness, there was also a lot of gratitude as my wedding day signified hope and the final realisation of my dream to become a mother. It was simply a sublime and heady day. I don't even remember the parts that weren't perfect (nothing is perfect), because I knew it was leading to a new and longed-for chapter in my life. My jaw ached by the end of it from smiling so much.

The result felt good, so I began to build up a 'happy bank'. I noticed that each feeling had a blueprint, allowing me to create a library of feelings and emotions and establish a deeper connection to my body. Every time I felt negative, anxious or stressed, I focused on these warm, all-encompassing feelings of joy, love, gratitude, excitement and passion inside me, long before I'd had time to think of a positive thought. I was still triggered daily (or hourly) by all the stresses and strains of modern living, but quickly turned my attention back to my heart and the feelings inside my happy bank. When I got annoyed, chanting a simple 'Om' mantra out loud helped to bring my vibrational resonance back to neutral (and out of anger) so I could return to the heart space again.

Like everything in life, the more I practised, the better I got. As I increasingly tuned in to my internal environment, focusing on the feelings in my heart and body, I began to feel different inside. In fact, I began to feel like a completely different person. That's when my life finally started to shift. I didn't know how to get out of my negative thinking (or depression) using my analytical brain, but using my feelings and emotions worked.

Little did I know that what I was doing was rewiring my mind to be positive via my feelings and emotions rather than my thoughts and deepening my connection to my energetic self. Feelings and thoughts work on a feedback loop. One affects the other. I had read about positive thinking, but like many of us, simply wasn't able to apply it. By approaching being positive via my feelings, I found what worked for me and was able to successfully apply this approach to help me change my life, personally and professionally, for the better. My entire life has changed beyond all recognition, simply because I learned to build on, and harness, these 'subtle energies'. Focusing on my feelings improved my intuition, perception and gut feelings, allowing me to harness my true energy and get me back to a happy state of being. It felt like I'd woken my energy up.

I'm a far happier mum these days and my husband and I are back to being best friends again – not because I'm making an external conscious effort, but because my mind has changed internally. I now approach everything from the inside out, checking with my feelings, mind, gut, energy, higher self and heart first and asking myself questions before I act. If I have a bad day and start to feel stressed, depressed or overwhelmed again, I know that I can just go inside myself and feel the warm, positive feelings to get myself back on track.

Introduction

Becoming a positive, 'feeling' person will change your life, but this is not a book about positive thinking. It's a book about your 'energy' and how positive feeling, combined with conscious intention, will help you more than you ever believed possible.

This book introduces you to the science behind the 'woo'. The gap between science and spiritual is gradually lessening as we learn more about the energetic universe and the multidimensional self. A knowledge of the power of you and the energetic world we live in is how you can turn your world upside down and transform your life from the inside out wherever you are.

Our brains create the reality of our lives. Whatever we are thinking about, we literally bring into being, because we are directing consciousness. Taking the time to step back and see how your thoughts could be affecting your life is a simple, but vital, act and something that busy, stressed people often forget to do. Do you know how long a person can keep a positive thought going? Not long, because we only operate from our 'thinking' mind around 5% of the time, which isn't long enough to make lasting changes.[1] We are also more disposed to thinking negatively as a way to keep us away from perceived risk. By approaching positivity via feelings instead of thoughts, we can keep the feeling going longer, because this action comes from the heart. You 'feel' better, not 'think' better. Essentially, we can bypass the mind (or ego), which often keeps us stuck in a low-vibrational state.

EXERCISE: Your Happiest Memory

Remember the happiest day of your life. What does it look like? What does it smell like? Can you visualise it? How do the memories make you feel?

Once you have found the perfect memory that evokes positive feelings of passion, gratitude and immense happiness, turn your attention to your heart. Feel those warm feelings inside your heart and then expand these warm, glowing and high-vibrational feelings outwards until you feel warm and glowing all over. Sit with these warm, loving feelings inside your heart for as long as you can.

Because you are rewiring your mind via your feelings, the more often you can do this simple exercise, the faster it will work. Both feelings and thoughts work on a feedback loop and the repetition changes you from within. It changes your subconscious mind, which is the part that you need to target if you are to make lasting changes.

We're not just affecting our thoughts; we're also changing our energies. Our feelings and emotions are energy. When we tap into our positive feelings, we are tapping into a massive amount of power that we can use for the benefit of ourselves and others. Our power is astounding, but by focusing too much on the external environment we are blinding ourselves to our true multidimensional and unlimited selves.

When you change your life from the inside out, you can feel it all – the energies inside you, your gut feelings and intuition that act as your internal compass, the absolute clarity and confidence you acquire when you know what you want and why you want it and the extreme creativity that will spark new and innovative ideas for your best life. When you come at your life from the inside out, you start to feel a fast shift as you step into the life that you truly want and begin to achieve your long-held dreams more easily. In fact, you won't look back.

This book can be read from beginning to end or you can skip around to find the information best suited to your needs in the moment. If you like science or you want 'proof', then the first three chapters will interest you. If you prefer spirit, phenomena and practical exercises to improve your life, then Chapters Four through Eight will probably interest you more. It's up to you how you read it – here is a chapter summary to help you decide.

Chapter One

This chapter explores energy in full: both 'low-vibrational' (contracted) energy and 'high-vibrational' (expanded) energy. It introduces the idea of vibrational frequencies and their importance. We learn that managing your emotions and feelings is the first step to harnessing the energetic world. This chapter introduces us to the unified (energy) field, consciousness, quantum entanglement, our electromagnetic field and various other terms in quantum physics as we look at the science behind how this stuff works.

Chapter Two

To truly raise our level of consciousness so we can experience a better life, we need to energetically work on our own minds and bodies. Epigenetics is the basis of this chapter, which delves more into the electromagnetic energy field that we exist in and into each cell in our body. We all have our own energy field (often referred to as our auric field, torus or even biofield), where a lot of information about us is held. Learning to understand and access this information can change your life.

Chapter Three

Creating our own reality by directing consciousness is the key to having a more abundant life. This chapter gives you the steps on how to do it. Being more intentional and knowing what you want puts you into the co-creator frequency, where you intentionally design your own life and business. Visualising it and keeping your vibrational frequency elevated are essential to success, because none of us can create or manifest from a place of lack, stress, impatience or negativity.

Chapter Four

This is where I share my thoughts on phenomena, in particular, my own experiences with my dead mother and my own child. I have a logical and rational mind, but I also trust myself (and my energy) implicitly and I knew I needed to explore these experiences. This chapter explores the idea of phenomena as information from the energy field, together with archetypal frequencies, that we can use to increase our understanding of ourselves and to improve our lives.

Chapter Five

Learning how to tap into consciousness and the energy field though meditation and my internal self has revolutionised my life. In this chapter, I teach you how to do it yourself. The higher your frequency, the more of an energetic upgrade you will receive and the better access you will have to the energy field and the higher vibrational frequencies that reside there.

Once we have learned how to tap into the energy field, we can discover what and how we can download or channel from it. The energy field consists of creativity, inspiration, knowledge, wisdom and information and we can access it all to find the answers to our questions, help us think creatively and channel inspiration and healing. You will learn that pushing yourself to work harder in life is not the way forward; tapping into your energy field shows you there is a better way.

Chapter Six

In this chapter, you will meet your superconscious (higher mind or higher self). This expanded version of your consciousness spans the entire universe and has access to all the wisdom and knowledge in it. We can get caught up with the physical body and forget that we also have access to higher wisdom. This chapter is full of exercises teaching you how to connect to your higher mind and find the answers to all the questions you have ever had about yourself and your business.

Chapter Seven

We can spend our lives 'manifesting' or creating and still not get the life we want to experience. This is because we are not working our energy correctly. Learning to tap into, and harness, our energy is crucial. In this chapter, we dive down deeper and learn how to work in flow while becoming more energetically aligned. Aligning our soul with our life and business creates more meaning, purpose and fulfilment. This creates more passion, drive, direction and motivation, while putting us back into a synchronistic state. Energetic alignment can change continuously, so this chapter gives you the tools you need to help you re-align yours as your life and business unfold.

Chapter Eight

We have to work in unity to improve our world for the next generation. We are all connected; what affects one person affects the rest. Find where you fit by being your authentic self. You can then start to vibrate at the frequency meant for you and start attracting people who are looking for you while managing your energy in a way that supports every aspect of your life. It really is that simple.

I hope you enjoy this book and find it useful. I wrote it because I wanted to give you hope and knowledge of a better world, and let people know that this better world is already inside us. Are you ready to energetically change your life and business for the better? It's simply a matter of learning how to access it – something that we should all have the opportunity to do.

ONE
Everything Is Energy

Discovering that I was made of energy really changed my perspective on life. At first, I found it unbelievable and didn't really understand how I could be energy. I kept poking my arm and thinking, 'But how can I be visible when energy is invisible?' but after the initial shock, this new perception served me well.

It allowed me to step outside my current reality and understand that I can change my life whenever I want to. It allowed me to look at myself and my life with a fresh perspective and childlike curiosity. For the first time in a long time, I felt free. I was no longer bound by my age, my gender, my location, my race, my financial situation, my experiences, my background, or even my marriage, because I could change it all inside. I was *energy*. I was free to do anything I wanted to in my life.

I woke up to the realisation that the only thing holding me back was me, or more specifically, my mind.

Ancient wisdom and cultures have known for centuries that we are made of energy. China has qi, India has prana, Japan has ki and ancient Egyptians had ka, to name a few. Their healing practices treated people as energetic beings, clearing away stagnation with therapies like acupuncture, yoga, tai chi or shamanistic practices. Unfortunately, the Western world was sceptical of these approaches because science couldn't easily explain how they worked.

This changed with quantum physics.

Quantum physics has been evolving since the 1800s and cannot be attributed to one scientist, but it is widely accepted that from circa 1900 Max Planck, Albert Einstein and Niels Bohr made some of the most significant contributions. Bohr and Planck each received a Nobel Prize in Physics for their work with quantum theory, which proposed that energy exists as discrete packets of energy known as quantum (plural quanta). Einstein won the 1921 Nobel Prize for his theory of the Photoelectric Effect where he described light as quanta.[2]

Quantum physics essentially studies the subatomic world and shows us how atoms work. In the 1920s, it incorporated quantum mechanics in the form of mathematical formula. This made things easier to understand.[3] In particular, Erwin Schrodinger, Werner

Heisenberg and others developed a concrete mathematical formula for the hydrogen atom. Previously, many scientists didn't believe atoms existed because they couldn't be seen, but the formula proved not only that they exist, but they are the building blocks of life.[4]

Minute particles exist inside the atom – protons and neutrons make up the nucleus, with electrons around the outside. Every particle (or group of particles) in the universe is also a wave (energy), and can occupy multiple places in space at once. This means that any chunk of matter can also occupy two places at once, a phenomenon physicists call 'quantum superposition'. During an experiment called the double-slit experiment it was found that we can observe these particles as matter before they were waves, often referred to as particle-wave duality or 'collapsing the wave' function.[5] This in turn created the 'observer effect' – in essence, the concept that matter (energy) is changed simply by being observed.[6] This is a fundamental part of quantum physics, and a fundamental part of this book, not because it's a book about quantum physics but because it's a book about observing your life and business dreams into reality; whatever they may be.

A particle such as an electron is not solid, but is made of energy, like tiny little vortexes. Since we are made up of these same particles, it means that we are the same: made of energy. You may wonder how we touch things or sit on our chair without falling through, but we don't really touch things in the physical sense. What we are experiencing is the push or force of the electromagnetic field around our atoms against the push or even 'dance' of the chair's atoms (electromagnetic field). In a sense, we are hovering slightly above the chair. It's our brain that provides us with the sensation of sitting down.

Our brain, or more specifically, our ego, is extremely adept at keeping us inside this reality we call the physical world, but this world is not really physical at all. What we think of as empty space isn't actually empty – it's full of energy. We live in a universe that is made of energy and matter is part of that field (or matrix) in the form of a potential or a possibility. Observing it brings it into our reality.

Everything is made from energy, so everything has its own vibrational frequency: you, the chair you are sitting on and even your words and feelings (which we will come back to in a bit). In quantum field theory, it's not that particles of matter come from these fields, it's that matter *is* these fields, in the form of a ripple, excitation or bundle of energy and everything exists in many different fields.[7] An easier way to understand this is to compare this field of energy to different states of mass. Energy is like a gas and matter is like a solid (eg, ice). Everything exists in the same field, but in different states. Plasma is a fourth state of matter that exists. Although it often behaves like a gas, it is not a gas, liquid or solid. According to Dr Dennis Gallagher, a plasma physicist at NASA's Marshall Space Flight Centre, '99.9% of the Universe is made up of plasma.'[8]

In Lynne McTaggart's book *The Field: The Quest for the Secret Force of the Universe,*[9] she refers to Karl Pibram's research on the brain and consciousness. Pibram believed that we perceive our physical reality by resonating with the quantum waves. McTaggart goes on to explain that our brains create the reality of the physical world around us based on the wavelengths (frequencies) that come in from the Field. Our memories are not held in our physical minds, but in our energetic minds. In a 2017 Ted Talk, neuroscientist Anil Seth explains that we 'hallucinate' the physical world around us and our brains create what we see; a bit like a 'virtual reality' game.[10]

As energetic beings made up of particles, we each have a unique frequency, just like we have our own, unique fingerprints. Although we are born with our unique frequency or vibrational resonance, it can change depending on our levels of consciousness (which we will come to in the next chapter) and through observing our own feelings, emotions, thoughts and even words.

Emotions as electrical charge

Emotions can be seen as a biochemical and electrical reaction to experiencing something. These bodily reactions can be measured a number of ways, including brain activity using an electroencephalogram (EEG) and heart rate via an electrocardiogram (ECG).[11] As this is an electrical response, it's producing electricity in the form of a light particle (photon) which we can measure or record. An emotion is actually neutral energy – it is the feeling (or belief) behind it that triggers a positive or negative response.

A feeling can be seen as the conscious experience of that biochemical response. We can consciously talk about our feelings – we may feel sad when we watch a sad movie or happy when we buy something new. We experience emotions and feelings from external experiences in our physical world, but this is not the only way we experience them. We also experience or feel them in our subconscious or energetic world. We are constantly surrounded by thoughts, frequencies (information), waves (energy) and consciousness, because this is what the energy field consists of. We'll come back to this when we discuss quantum entanglement.

Because it has an electric charge, the electromagnetic field can be measured in hertz frequency. (There are many images of a 'hertz frequency of emotions table' online if you want to see a visual representation). Feelings such as anger, grief and apathy are at the lower end of the frequency spectrum and can be referred to as 'low-vibrational frequencies' and feelings such as love, compassion and peace are at the higher end and can be referred to as 'high-vibrational frequencies'. These higher vibrational feelings can also be felt inside us as expanded energy, as opposed to lower vibrational ones that feel contracted. Contracted feels small, scared or

narrow. Expanded makes us feel big, alive and connected.[12]

How many of us recognise that we are more than our
feelings or emotions? I know I didn't, which is why
I sat in depression for decades. My mum had been
depressed, so I thought that it was just part of my
genes. I accepted it as part of who I was. How wrong I
was. Once I started to explore the energetic universe, it
became a life-changing journey. I can now see that life
isn't about feelings and emotions, it's about your state
of being (your level of consciousness); and although it's
not an overnight thing, we can change this by ourselves
(the next chapter will show you how).

Your unique vibrational frequency can be dictated by
your mood, emotions and feelings, but it can also be
dictated by your belief structures, level of consciousness, perception and even by your behaviour (because
how we act is a result of how we feel). You are constantly broadcasting a vibrational frequency and even
the words that you use can affect the outcome of your
life. I can think of two good examples of this. First is
how long your house plants live for: they will thrive if
you talk lovingly to them, but they will wither away
if you completely ignore them (like I used to). Second
is Masaru Emoto's snowflake theory, which shows us
that saying loving words to water before turning it into
snow creates beautiful symmetrical patterns, whereas
saying angry or cruel words creates ugly and disjointed

patterns.[13] This shows us the power of loving words, whether they are spoken to others or to ourselves.

It's not just the emotions that you feel inside you that affect your energetic field, it's also the sensory experiences or subtle energies that come from outside of you (or even thoughts that wash over you) that result in an emotional response. Understanding this completely revolutionised my life because I had been pulled sideways by them for decades. We must first understand our own feelings and emotions, though.

In addition to the sensory 'feelings' or subtle energies that come from outside you, there are the ones that you have because of something that has happened which your body needs to recognise. If you like, the feelings are your body communicating with you and giving you conscious information, while your emotions act as a 'snapshot' of your life, storing the electrical charge in your subconscious mind (or even body).[14] The storage and release of these electrical charges is the basis of energy work, which is how you can transform your life in minutes when you release any trapped or 'stuck' energy. We will come back to this in the next chapter when we look at epigenetics and our belief structures.

When you take back control of your feelings, you take back control of your life. Understanding that we are continuously vibrating as we move in and out of our feelings and emotions is the key to harnessing our power. Emotions are the energy that drives us. We can control this energy, which means we can also control our feelings and emotions. Difficult people or stressful situations can affect our mood for hours, days, or even years, but when we understand that these feelings are simply fleeting moments, we can control them and life gets better. We only feel a feeling for around ninety seconds (known as the 90-second rule), but we find ourselves held hostage by them as they dictate our lives.[15]

Understanding that we are merely energy vibrating at certain frequencies gives us immense control over our lives because we are no longer led by our feelings. We can feel them, hear their message, act accordingly and let them go: they are a 'call to action' or message from our body telling us to act. We're still human though, so if it's a strong negative emotion that results in a negative charge or state of being, then we know that we have stumbled onto something bigger. It could be a limiting belief, incorrect perception or a deep-rooted insecurity. Good indicators here are things that trigger you. When you get triggered by something or someone, explore it with tools such as journaling or meditation and feel into what that stuck emotion (belief) is. What is your body or mind trying to tell you? We can work on ourselves with journaling, meditation and Emotional Freedom Technique (EFT or Tapping) to work it through and out of our system. I will come back to these techniques in full later.

Dr Bruce Lipton, a stem cell biologist and author of three bestselling books,[16] talks about 'good vibrations' and how, on a molecular level, our energy is always gravitating towards other energy that is in harmony with it. Because of constructive interference – the phenomenon where two waves become in-phase and the amplitude of the combined waves is equal to the sum of the individual ones[17] – we know that when two harmonious energies come together, they create a good vibe and more energy. Animals are still guided in this way, which we often call intuition or extrasensory perception (ESP), but as humans we have developed language and words, so we don't do this anymore. We have stopped trusting our bodies and have started trusting other people over ourselves. Our bodies can tell us when something (or someone) is not quite right for us and when we listen and tune into these bodily vibrations, we connect to an entire world that is talking to us all the time.[18]

I believe that these subtle vibrations or vibrational energies that we are made of and surrounded by hold the key to our success in the material world. Here is a simple way you can start to understand more of these subtleties. Find a quiet space where you won't be distracted, and simply sit in silence. Even if you can only manage five minutes and you're sitting in your car in the car park, sit in the stillness and quiet and open yourself to the possibilities. The more you listen and feel into your inner world, the more aware you will become of it. It's that awareness that we want to harness.

We are essentially consciousness living in a 'physical' body, and consciousness is awareness, according to the *Oxford Advanced Learner's Dictionary*.[19] The more aware you become of your body and those subtle energies and feelings, the faster your world will change, because you are increasing your connection to the energy field and the frequencies or information that lives 'in' there. You'll find you'll be so aware of your inner world that you'll know instantly when something feels out of sync or unaligned either with yourself or the people around you. You will start to become the 'observer' of your life, and this changes everything. These days, I can do this as I hang out the washing or walk around the house, but our energy's 'voice' is subtle, which is how I managed to ignore it for decades.

Energy (or to be more precise, consciousness) is information, which we can decipher using all our senses, not just the five physical ones. Our inner world is full of intuitive hunches, energetic sensations and vibrations, because we are electric beings. They are also in the energy field around us, but as these are invisible, we can't access them with our physical bodies or senses (although we're developing new technology every day that can record them). We can only access them with our awareness or inner sense. Unfortunately, many people are in denial of both these and their true energetic natures. They believe that if we can't see them, then they're not there, but they are and we can tap into them for our own benefit.

Our electromagnetic energy field

Although we live in a unified field containing the electromagnetic energy field, every single thing has its own electromagnetic field around it (also called the aura or Torus field). Remember the chair repelling you so that you don't actually sit on it but your atoms hover slightly above it? Well, these atoms all have their own electromagnetic field around them too, which not only hold, and share, information with each other but also make up part of the energetic environment that we exist in. The understanding of our electromagnetic energy field in terms of health and wellness has opened up many new areas, such as energy medicine and biofield science, an 'emerging field of study that aims to provide a scientific foundation for understanding the complex homeodynamic regulation of living systems'.[20] Our bodies are lots of little atomic electromagnetic energy fields or light packets, gravitationally joined together to create us.[21] These little fields of energy are filled with information, which comes from our mouths as we speak, our thoughts as we think, our perceptions based on what we believe, what we watch on TV or experience in our 'environment' and our emotions based on how we feel. And this is where the problem lies for many of us.

Our environment is not just the information that comes from the physical cells – it's also the information that comes from the energetic (invisible) aspects of our cells. Every time we speak, we fill these cells with high-vibrational energy or low-vibrational energy, which is frequency.[22] Our electromagnetic energy field is a bit like having our own 'cloud storage' because it holds a lot of data about our physical, emotional, mental, spiritual and environmental selves. This information can be positive or detrimental to us and we can literally be weighed down with the 'negativity' of past experiences.

The energetic space between the atoms and molecules should ideally be as 'clear' or high-vibrational as possible so that consciousness can flow through from the energy field and animate us, bringing us to life and keeping us balanced and healthy. However, in our current low-density world, much of this space is taken up with negative, trapped emotions in the form of memories and beliefs which are blocking the energy from running through our meridian centres and bodies. Without consciousness flowing through us, life feels limited and we start to become less energetic and expanded in nature.

Our bodies have a natural frequency that they prefer to vibrate at. This is governed by our electromagnetic field. When we are in resonance with this frequency, the body is strong and in harmony with all levels, so we are healthy and energetically aligned. When we have blockages or stagnation in our field, the frequency is disrupted and we lose homeostasis or balance. We take our bodily lifeforce from our own electromagnetic energy field, so when we feel burnt-out, our electromagnetic field has, in fact, burnt out. If we don't work on recharging and replenishing it, we could end up getting sick, ageing faster and generally feeling down, exhausted or even depressed. Stress burns us out because it keeps us continuously in the 'fight or flight' state, and yet we are living in constant stress these days (even in our dreams, as we wake up at 3am worrying about our 'to do' list or how we will pay the bills). This is why self-care is so important.

By far the quickest way to recharge it is through our own heartfelt feelings. The HeartMath Institute have been studying the heart for decades and have shown that out of all of these electromagnetic energy fields in our bodies, the heart is the strongest. It is 100 times stronger than the brain's magnetic field.[23] We don't replenish our bodies with the mind – we replenish them with the heart. I think on an intuitive level we know this, because we can feel that overthinking, overplanning and trying to find solutions to our problems with the mind often doesn't work. It just makes us feel more exhausted and more burnt-out. Leading from the heart in our lives and business not only allows us to follow the right path for us (the wisdom of the heart) but it also keeps us healthier, happier and more fulfilled. Our own electromagnetic energy field is said to stretch up to 9ft outside of our bodies, but if yours is diminished then it will be less and there will be less high-vibrational energy to create a more thriving business and life.[24] We can recharge it by spending more time every day sitting in high-frequency feelings of love, compassion, excitement, inspiration, gratitude, self-love, enthusiasm, joy and passion.

Quantum entanglement theory

Quantum entanglement theory was discovered in the mid-1900s. It is a remarkable phenomenon and, along with the energy (quantum) field, the observer effect, consciousness and vibrational frequency or resonance, makes up much of this book. When scientists split a particle inside an atom, they saw that each half reacted in the same way when they interfered with the other half. It didn't matter what happened to the particle, or how far away they were, the same thing happened to its twin.[25]

The European Organisation for Nuclear Research, or CERN Institute, in Geneva has an atom-splitting machine and has been studying phenomena like this for years.[26] They've shown how we are all connected to each other through quantum entanglement theory. It is thought that when the Big Bang created our universe, it split matter and this matter then went on to create everything else in our universe, including us. We already know that the atoms in the human body are traceable to stars that exploded billions of years ago.[27] Although we are all made from particles that have been split, we were once all connected, so we work from the same principle: what happens to one particle happens to all.

We are all energetically connected to each other through quantum entanglement, whether we are aware of it or not. How many times have you said something at the exact same time as someone else? How many times have you finished someone's sentence? How many times have you gone to phone someone only to have them call you? These are all examples of entanglement. As soon as you think of someone or focus your attention on something or someone, you become energetically entangled with their field. It's because of entanglement theory that we can work energetically with people anywhere in the world with methods like quantum reiki or over Zoom.

I think we all know that feeling of walking into an office or room with negative energy in it. The second we step foot in the door, our energy drops and we start to feel down or we become angry or sad for no apparent reason.

It's important to find a place where your energy can thrive. This in turn will help you thrive. We are always being told to be aware of who we spend our time with, but in reality, we are surrounded by energy, both high- and low-vibrational frequencies every day. You don't necessarily need to delete low-vibrational people from your life; you can instead work on raising your own frequency and 'sealing' your auric field with energy techniques. I have first-hand experience of this within my marriage. Both my husband and I were depressed after our mothers died within a year of each other. For a while, I honestly didn't know how to improve things and we just argued and lived out our inherited stories and patterns for years. Eventually, I discovered that working hard on increasing my own frequency by expanding my heartfelt emotions outward had a positive effect on him, too. As we entangled with each other, he is now more positive and back to himself. Of course, being more conscious of my own actions and words helps too, which we will come back to in the next chapter.

You can also use this 'heart expanding' method when you go to events, meetings or parties – anywhere that involves socialising or interacting with others. As you walk into the room, focus on expanding your heartfelt feelings out of your body, radiating warmth outwards. You will be amazed at the difference it makes in the room. People will be drawn to you and your elevated energy. If you can't feel those warm feelings, then just think about something or someone you love and feel passionate about. It doesn't matter where the love comes from, it only matters that you feel it inside you and expand it outwards from your heart into the energy field around you.

Consciousness

Consciousness is energy. We view consciousness as the 'energetic part' of us (often called the soul), but in reality, we are all part of this intuitive, intelligent and animated essence that is consciousness. In fact, consciousness has been described as the thing that underpins everything, even the subatomic (quantum) field, largely because consciousness is seen as the ultimate 'observer' and observes matter into being. As new research is showing that consciousness can pre-empt our thoughts and expectations – showing that we can direct it – many of us are now beginning to see that learning to harness or work with consciousness is the key to creating a better life for ourselves.

What exactly is consciousness? No one knows for sure, but there are a lot of people researching it, especially in the fields of Artificial Intelligence (AI). Some scientists think it's generated by the brain's own electromagnetic energy field[28] and others believe the brain is not a generator of consciousness but rather a receiver of it from the energy field around us.[29] Stanislav Grof, a psychiatrist and researcher of consciousness, stated that the brain is more like a physical 'reducing valve', acting as a conduit for consciousness. It allows our brains not to be overwhelmed by the infinite field of energy around us so we can filter out what we don't need.[30] Bernardo Kastrup, a computer engineer and author, believes that hallucination is not the overstimulation of the brain as we once thought, but rather the opposite. The brain has 'reduced' its connection to the physical world and so is now more connected to the energy field or consciousness around us for a more expanded version of reality.[31] The brain is like a computer or hard drive processing information 'downloaded' from the energy field.[32] This not only indicates that what we see in our hallucinations may be 'real', but also that connecting to higher consciousness in this 'mystical' but spiritual way can heal our mind, as studies into psilocybin (magic mushrooms) on depression are also indicating.[33]

The Orch OR theory devised by Stuart Hameroff and Roger Penrose states that the brain acts like a quantum mechanical computer and consciousness is woven into the brain. Quantum vibrations in tiny proteins called microtubules are found inside brain neurons, showing us that consciousness may indeed be quantum and coming from the energy field 'around' us.[34] When we become more connected to the energy field, we can sense or experience more of our 'inner world' or consciousness (our energy) in the form of subtle vibrations, intuitions, sensations and knowing. As more of us wake up to this energetic side of ourselves, we are evolving as a species. It's always been there – we just weren't aware of it. Maybe this is the next generation for humans: moving into our true super-minds and connecting with other frequencies and dimensions around us in a way that helps us thrive?

Another area of research on consciousness is near-death experiences (NDEs). This makes sense, as it is at this point that our consciousness or energy leaves our physical body. Peter Fenwick, neuropsychiatrist, neurophysiologist and the author of *The Art of Dying*[35] has been studying near-death cases for decades, as has Raymond Moody, who wrote *Life After Life: The Bestselling Original Investigation That Revealed Near-Death Experiences*,[36] Eben Alexander, who wrote *Proof of Heaven: A Neurosurgeon's Journey into the Afterlife*[37] and Dr Pim van Lommel, a cardiologist and author of *Consciousness Beyond Life: The Science of the Near-Death Experience*.[38]

In NDE studies, thousands of people have been interviewed. There are some remarkable similarities in their stories, such as interviewees being able to see and hear conversations happening in the operating rooms and even hearing and seeing conversations several miles down the road. When the subjects wake from surgery, they give such vivid accounts of activities that they could only have heard or seen these if they had been there. Some can even describe what people were wearing, who was there and what private conversations they were having. In the physical world we see and hear things using our five senses, but if we are clinically dead (our brain has not only 'flatlined', but there is no electrical activity at all) then we no longer have access to those senses. Dr van Lommel explores how these people could have seen or heard conversations and concludes that our consciousness or awareness can transcend our physical bodies in a way that we don't yet fully understand.

As tens of thousands of NDE recovering patients suggest, consciousness doesn't need a physical body to exist. So where does our consciousness go when we die? Most likely back into the energy field around us. In an interview with Peter Fenwick, he reports multiple people who describe integrating back into the cosmos again, which makes sense when you consider consciousness is energy and energy is consciousness and they cannot exist without each other.[39] When the talented Steve Jobs died, his last words were reported to be, 'Oh wow, oh wow, oh wow.'[40]

Consciousness never dies because it is energy and energy cannot be destroyed. It simply changes state. When we tap into this vast field of energy (also known as the unified or zero-point field), we do so for our own benefit. We can tap into the consciousness of others, and in theory, even people who have 'died'. After my mother died, I could feel her energy and even heard her voice, but I am not a medium. These are all phenomena that many of us have felt after the passing of loved ones. We can't explain it, but we still feel their presence. The concept of consciousness and the energy field provides me with a good explanation.

Remote viewing is a phenomenon studied by many scientists. Known as Project Star Gate, the US military also researched it and had an operational unit used to determine the locations of various military bases around the world and even on other planets.[41] Remote viewing is a prime example of 'quantum entanglement' or what is referred to as nonlocality.[42] In my opinion, remote viewing is probably the best way of understanding consciousness, because not only does it show that consciousness can see (have an awareness of) independently of our own eyes, but also that everything is connected in the energy field or universe – even physical matter.

In the end, we are all connected to each other in some way or another. If you have ever felt that you weren't reaching your full potential but couldn't figure out why, then the next chapter is for you.

TWO

Our Beliefs Create Our Reality

In the last chapter, we talked about how our feelings and emotions can dictate our unique frequency. Our perceptions, state of being, belief structure and our level of consciousness also affect our unique frequency.

Everything (including the brain) has an electromagnetic energy field around it which holds data about us. Our brains are not able to hold much data. In a 2017 TED Talk, cognitive scientist Philip Fernbach shares the results of an experiment by a psychologist named Thomas Landauer in the 1980s to estimate the size of an individual's knowledge base in bytes. Using his data, he was able to estimate the rate at which we can acquire knowledge and also the rate at which we forget what we learn. He then extrapolated to a seventy-year lifespan. His estimate of how much we know? 1GB. We are just not made to store a lot of detailed information.[43]

No one really knows where we store or pull our memories from, but when you consider that they are held in our own 'cloud storage' or energetic field, it makes sense. We energetically hold them in the brain's energy field, which can be seen as the mind. The conscious part of our mind can be viewed as our 'thinking' mind because we are aware of the thoughts that come out of it. Our subconscious mind, on the other hand, is a feeling mind. We are not consciously aware of what's in our subconscious mind, but because it's part of the autonomic nervous system, it never switches off. Most people operate from the subconscious mind around 90–95% of the time but are largely unaware of this.[44] The subconscious is linked directly to our feelings and emotions and can be thought of as the 'mind' of the body, or even the electromagnetic field of the body. While these feelings and emotions – in the form of memories and beliefs – can be positive, they can also be our personal saboteurs, as they contain our pre-programming from childhood and may even be passed down from previous generations (we will explore this later). The only way we can step out of the limitations of this part of our mind is to explore it, understand it and then rewire it.

Rewiring the neural pathways is a field of study known as neuroplasticity. Neuroplasticity essentially refers to the brain's ability to delete old or redundant neural connections and form new neural pathways. We can physically change our old beliefs or habits, including those that we built up in childhood, through this process as our brain works on deleting the old pathways and focuses on building new ones.[45]

Our minds work on a feedback loop with our emotions and are intertwined. What we think, we feel. This means that our thoughts and feelings broadcast out of our minds and energy fields all the time, often causing us to react irrationally. How many times have we shouted at someone and then walked away thinking, 'Where did that come from?' When I snap at the kids or my husband, I push myself into 'observer' mode afterwards so I can try and understand what triggered me. Being in observer mode is another way of saying 'becoming more conscious'. Essentially, being more aware or conscious pulls us back from our subconscious 'stuff' and allows us to consciously see how we are acting towards the people around us. It allows us to view our lives from a bird's eye view so we can see how things are really playing out.

Accessing our subconscious mind

Our subconscious mind broadcasts frequencies that, most of the time, we are not even aware of. As we operate from our subconscious mind most of the time, this can be problematic. How can we know what frequency we are broadcasting? Relaxing and focusing on changing our beta brainwaves to alpha brainwaves takes us out of the beta, 'physical world', brainwave state and, by default, out of the physical world 'chatter' and distractions. Once we have relaxed and switched ourselves off from the stress of the outer world, we can begin to access our subconscious mind by simply asking ourselves questions. The challenge is making sense of the information once we have accessed it.

The questions are important and you may need to think outside of the box to find ones that work for you. Often, just rephrasing the questions we ask our subconscious mind can make a massive difference to understanding what is holding us back in life. Here are a couple of simple exercises you can do now to begin accessing your subconscious:

EXERCISE: Discover Your Limiting Beliefs

Start a journal, writing down all the things that you want more clarity on. Focus on things you want in order to understand why you haven't achieved them yet. Ask yourself questions such as:

- Why haven't I achieved the success I want yet?
- What is stopping me from achieving the health, prosperity or fulfilling relationship I want?
- Why haven't I met my life partner yet?
- What do I want my life to look like?
- What are my biggest life dreams?

- What is it I want but haven't gotten yet?
- What is the business of my dreams?
- Why am I not attracting my ideal clients?

The clues are in what your dreams are made of. Take a look at where you want to be, and why you haven't gotten there yet. This is where your limiting beliefs lie. Continue to journal to explore your subconscious and find out what these beliefs are. The more you journal, the more clarity and understanding you will get.

EXERCISE: Find the Obstacles to Your Goals

Find a quiet place to sit down and relax. Take a deep breath and close your eyes as you exhale. Pull your attention to the middle of your head and focus on the space behind your eyes, where your pineal gland is located. Now ask yourself what it is you really want.

Write down the first three goals that come into your head for the coming year and journal on why you want to achieve them. The answers are always in the why.

Now, feel into these reasons.

- Do they resonate?
- Does your heart feel happy with them?
- Do you feel true desire in achieving them?

Don't think too far ahead and try to strategise them, plan them or even be logical about them – that comes later. First, you need to understand where they come from: your heart, your ego or your subconscious pre-programming.

> Once you have understood what you want from your year ahead, ask yourself what is stopping you from achieving it. When you become good at this (which you will), you will be surprised how much your mind can relay back to you. You will start to have truly enlightening dialogues with yourself on a daily basis that will help you in so many ways.

There will always be fear when examining the things that hold you back, but try and find out where the fear is coming from. For example, when I first started writing this book, there was a lot of fear and confusion around the content, how it fitted into my business, and even who I was writing it for. I knew that many people would think it was a bit 'out there', but I could feel the strong desire and drive coming from my heart and knew that this was a goal that I really wanted to achieve: I passionately feel this will help more people live better lives. Eliminate 'should' goals, 'could' goals and goals around money for now and start with something simple. Ask yourself, 'What would I feel proud at having achieved when I reach the end of this year?'

I used to have crippling self-doubt for years before I finally understood that I was stopping myself from even seeing my dreams. It never occurred to me that I could have them. I subconsciously thought that I couldn't have what I really wanted in life, so my mind didn't even bother recognising them as a possibility. Eventually, I started to 'think big'. I transcended my limitations and pushed myself into a magical fantasy world where I could have anything I wanted and then I used this to come back down to earth armed with the answers I needed.

Our beliefs about ourselves and the world we live in create our reality. We are, quite literally, our beliefs. Imagine that you are wearing a virtual reality mask and its filters are all the beliefs and perceptions (known and unknown) that you have built up in your life. That's how we view the world. As you can imagine, this can massively limit our lives, as we are looking at the world around us based on what we perceive to be true. Our lives become what we believe or expect them to be (belief leads to expectation), which can limit us or free us depending on our thoughts. Thanks to neuroplasticity, we can change these old beliefs, stories and pre-programming, but to change them forever, we need to add a positive or high-vibrational feeling into the mix. This is how positive affirmations and mantras work, but you must feel the positive feeling from within your heart and body. We will come back to this in a lot more detail as we go through the book.

We are continuously projecting our beliefs out into the world and we see what we believe we are going to see. If we think that the world is unfair, then that is what we will see and we will continue to live in an unfair world until we change our beliefs around it. When I first started energy therapy, I discovered that one of my ingrained limiting beliefs was that 'life is unfair'.

This was most likely determined in my childhood, and although there were positive aspects too, I am amazed how much this has shaped my life: ranging from a saviour complex to being a victim, to undercharging, to low self-esteem and even being sacked from jobs.

Beliefs go far deeper than that, though. We get told we are lazy or bad at maths, so we become lazy and bad at maths. Many of our current beliefs around who we are come from the inherited programming from our family, friends, cultures, societies, schools, jobs and even ancestors, and were never ours in the first place. A 2017 article in the *London Evening Standard* noted that the UK teaches maths in a way that is too complex for the children to grasp and overloads them with information.[46] This introduces an inherent lack of confidence around the subject and these children grow up believing that they can't do maths, which isn't true. As you can imagine, this doesn't bode well for financial freedom or understanding money later on in life.

We recently started home-schooling our children because of my son's learning difficulties and my daughter's apparent struggle. Before we left the school, I sat down with my seven-year-old daughter's teacher, who informed me that my child wasn't academic, but she loved fashion, so maybe she could go to college and do something along those lines. As I walked away, I knew in my heart that my daughter can be anything she sets her mind to. The teacher meant well, but he didn't have awareness of his own limiting beliefs, which created this well-meaning assumption in the first place. My daughter may well end up doing something in fashion, because she does love fashion and designing new outfits, but she also loves gymnastics, dancing, food, films, singing and shares my love of coaching and teaching too. All these passions of hers are simply self-expression and creativity flowing through her, as we will explore in Chapter Five. Her success will come from the direction and focus of this self-expression (her energy), so it is a far more complex equation than simply how 'academic' she is at school. I failed all my A levels (even getting a U in English Literature) but I've still managed to do OK in my life.

The interesting thing about limiting beliefs is that we can't see them and we certainly don't know how they are holding us back. They are our blind spot, and just like the blind spot in our car where we can't see another car coming up behind us, we also can't see how we are tripping ourselves up. Everyone else can though.

Before the age of seven, we believe everything we see and hear and are literally not conscious. We live in a state of theta and alpha brainwaves, which are also the hypnotic brainwaves and are always open to suggestion.[47] Theta is also the brainwave responsible for imagination, which we will come back to in Chapter Four. This is Mother Nature's way of helping us to learn – we simply 'download' (energetically) all this information from our environment, parents, siblings, school, friends, TV, films, books, etc. We absorb it all and take it as gospel. Around our seventh birthday, we enter into the 'age of reason', a term that signifies a period of neurological growth in the temporal and frontal lobes. We step into life as a conscious person and the analytical (and questioning) mind kicks in. Everything we learned before the age of seven or eight becomes our programming for the rest of our life, except that was never our programming to begin with – it belongs to everyone else.

In our home-schooling environment, we teach our children lots of things to help them override negative or unhelpful conditioning, such as about pseudo-truths in advertising, critical thinking, rewards for self-belief, keeping a gratitude journal, pompom points for positive self-talk and, of course, learning about our true intuitive self and inner wisdom. I feel that learning about their inner voice and how to trust and believe in themselves are hugely important life skills so that they don't end up following the crowd into trouble when they are teenagers or beyond. We all have this internal compass that guides us through life, but if we can't hear it (or we ignore it) then we will end up having to learn through experience instead. Looking back at my twenties and teenage years (and wondering how I ever made it out alive) I don't think I want my children to go down that route. Although I know that teenagers and young adults need to explore life, I feel safer knowing that they are exploring it with a strong sense of self and an inner understanding of what (and who) feels right and wrong to them.

Epigenetics

Epigenetics is a new biology based around our genes and deoxyribonucleic acid (DNA). In 1942, Conrad Waddington introduced the term and defined it as the 'whole complex of developmental processes' that lie between genotype and phenotype, although the usage and meaning has changed drastically since then.[48] In the 1970s it became popular again and studies began looking at environmental factors such as smoking and psychological factors such as studying identical twins (who are identical on a DNA level, but then change physically and behaviourally as they grow) and epigenetics is now a widely researched area.[49]

Scientists such as Dr Bruce Lipton discovered that our genes are switched on by our environment, so what we thought were genes that we can't change (turning us into victims of our birth) turns out not to be the case. Our environment can be viewed as anything from where we live, to who we hang out with, to what we eat, our lifestyle, what we believe, how we behave, think, speak, feel and more. Essentially, what Dr Lipton says is that our genes can be turned on or off by the information held in our own electromagnetic energy field, which also includes our beliefs.[50]

The power of our minds (and beliefs) is incredible. One great example of this is the placebo effect in the health sector, where the patient believes a sugar pill is healing them, so it does. Dr Lipton also discusses the nocebo effect, where negative beliefs can do the opposite.[51] In my heart, I feel that this is why both my mother and mother-in-law died earlier than they should have. My mother did smoke, but they were both extremely unfulfilled in life and not only suffered from debilitatingly low self-esteem (negative beliefs) but also from negative thinking and bouts of depression. There is much research available on positive thinking, but in my personal journey I have discovered that positive *feeling* works even better, as it is far easier to do. It's hard to change the mind, but it's easy to feel the heart.

Research is increasingly supporting the notion that epigenetic changes to our DNA can be passed down through generations.[52] So, perhaps many of us are stuck in the groove that our ancestors created.

Self-limiting beliefs

For example, if you want to find out if you have limited thinking around money, then simply ask yourself, 'Am I earning the money that I want to earn?' If the answer is no, then you are probably sabotaging yourself in this area. The more you worry, stress or feel anxious and desperate about money, the more money 'stories' (saboteurs) you most likely have. Remember, the self-sabotaging answers always lie in what your dreams are made of, so what do you want? Start exploring why you are not currently earning the money that you want. I had a lot of blocks around money and had to work hard on finding them – things like believing I could only earn money through marriage or that men make the money and women don't. These were extremely ingrained into my maternal family line, and were also linked to feelings of low self-worth, so I had to tackle both areas at the same time. They still come up, which is why it's a lifelong journey (although it gets easier) and I can see that a lot of the arguments I have had with my husband are because of these money stories.

There are seven main limiting beliefs around money that most of us share. Consider if you have limiting beliefs around the areas below:

1. There isn't enough money to go around (making us compete for it).

2. Money is evil (only evil people are rich).

3. We have to work extremely hard to make money.

4. Men earn the money (downplaying females).

5. It's hard to hold onto money (turns us into consumerists and materialists).

6. I'm not worthy of money (we block ourselves from receiving it).

7. Money is not important (we feel guilty for focusing on making it or wanting it).

Clearing away these old beliefs from my energy field helped me to release trapped energy (in the form of emotions) and the way I thought about money, which in turn helped me to step into a more abundant and prosperous life. This new awareness also increased my levels of consciousness, which not only makes me healthier and boosts my immune system, but makes me feel happier too. By bringing these old, incorrect beliefs into my conscious mind, I was able to see them, process them and release them. Limiting beliefs can stack up in your auric field, affecting the flow of energy coming in from the energy field and through the meridian channels and chakras in your body. The more you work on eliminating false beliefs from your field, the more you open yourself up to the full potential of the energy field (abundance) and the less you will self-sabotage.

Some of us can be exceptionally good at creating (manifesting) what we want, but how often do we then mess it up? As I look back at my own life, I see so many opportunistic situations that felt magical at the time, but ended up with me sabotaging them a few months later. If I hadn't taken the time to explore this, I know I would still be 'unconsciously' doing this. These days it's easier to achieve, as energy work means that we can explore and deal with things far quicker than more traditional methods.

What we see as unresolved issues or emotional baggage isn't anything more than just energy and we can literally blow it away. How? In the same way that we can energetically build up false beliefs from our environment and store them in our energy field as emotions, we can also energetically remove them. This is the basis of energy work such as breathwork, quantum touch and other focused breathing techniques. Breathwork can blow or breathe out the trapped, stagnating energy (emotions and beliefs), although they may come back if the subconscious mind hasn't accepted the changes too, which we will come back to later. Every time we remove a limiting belief from our mind, we are also changing our DNA, changing our frequency and thus changing our future. When we 'remove' an old or inherited limiting belief that has been around for decades, we release energy, or frequency, from our bodies. By releasing these old energies, we create space for more positive energies that are more aligned with where we want to be personally and professionally. Working on and eliminating a limiting belief creates a gap where more of the potential of the energy field can enter into your life, creating more abundance. Releasing a limiting belief allows the release of low-vibrational energy so your body's overall energetic resonance is raised into a higher frequency or level of consciousness.

Releasing limiting beliefs

Epigenetics shows that our DNA changes throughout our life and works on a feedback system with ribonucleic acid (RNA) and proteins. Although our genetic code doesn't change, the expression of this code changes, which can feed back into our body and upgrade our DNA. Our beliefs (via the emotions they create) can affect the proteins in the body, which feed back to the RNA, and then DNA and back again, continuously. The nucleus of the DNA is like the brain, giving instructions and holding the long-term memories built up over time; duly passing them on to each generation.[53] We are all connected to the quantum field via our cellular proteins, DNA and our energy fields, and work in harmony with it. Consciousness is an energy field that can affect and control the proteins in our body. It is the environment.[54] Essentially, consciousness continually upgrades our body, or at least the high-vibrational energies do, which we will come back to in more detail as we work through the book.

We can inherit beliefs from our ancestors, too. When you think about it, this makes perfect sense. We inherit 'programming' from our parents to help us learn the multitude of things that we need to know to keep us safe on this planet.[55] They inherited this knowledge from their parents. When we entangle with our parents' or friends' energy fields, we download information from them as well, helping us stay in the tribe and learn from others. You may have heard the phrase, 'We are the average of the five people we spend the most time with.' This is how I managed to work on my husband's happiness: via my own. Our beliefs change our DNA and can reprogramme us. (Whether the change is to a better way of living depends on the beliefs. If your beliefs are no longer true for you, they may not be improving your life.)

Thoughts are energy. Waves (energy) and particles are interchangeable at the quantum level. Most of our environment comes from our own electromagnetic energy field, which is where our memories, beliefs, thoughts and emotions lie. Changing our energy field changes our environment, because it changes our unique frequency. We achieve this through our own minds (and hearts). Our minds are incredibly powerful, as you will find out in the next chapter.

By unpicking our beliefs about ourselves, we can change everything and anything; we can even delay the ageing process. More research is going into this area but it's looking like certain aspects of ageing come about because we believe or think they will.[56] Science is now beginning to understand ageing from a molecular basis, making this an area that many industries are already researching as we continue our societal obsessions with turning back the clock and immortality. Every day, humans are doing amazing things to raise our collective levels of consciousness that shatter our currently limited thinking, such as when Roger Bannister ran the four-minute mile. It had been widely accepted that it was impossible to do, so no one even bothered to try. Once he proved it was possible, he broke our collective limiting beliefs around it, leading the way for more runners to do the same (the first of which was only forty-six days later by John Landy in Finland). There are even records of a herbalist in China called Li Ching-Yuen living to the age of 256 years.[57] It doesn't matter if you believe it or not, just by reading this statement you have now changed your perception, awareness or beliefs about ageing. Is it really possible to live until the age of 256? Who knows, but why don't you try anyway? Why limit yourself?

A common catchphrase in the last century was, 'You are what you eat.' A popular catchphrase for this century is, 'You are what you believe you are.' When you grasp this concept, it really is the start of your new life and I urge you to embrace it with both arms. Working on changing your beliefs is never going to be wasted work and the more you do it, the better, happier, healthier, younger and more successful you will feel. So much of my 'personality' turned out not to be mine at all and interests such as cooking, sewing, women's magazines and fashion I can now see either belonged to my mother or the collective consciousness. I have spent the past two years rediscovering the real me and I highly recommend you do the same. It's so liberating to find out who you really are without the 'pull' of the collective.

How can we begin the process of changing our DNA for the better? It's as simple as thinking more positively on a daily basis, but as many of us find this hard to do because of negative thinking, stress and hidden saboteurs in our subconscious mind, the growing world of energy therapies and medicine can help.

Energy work

Since the 1980s, we have seen an increase in energy therapies like energy psychology. These therapies combine Eastern and Western approaches by working with people on both their belief structures and their energy. Energy therapy was initially created by Roger Callahan PhD in the early 1980s and called Thought Field Therapy.[58] It was further developed by David Feinstein PhD, a clinical psychologist. There are now several branches of this practice, including Thought Field Therapy (TFT), Emotional Freedom Technique (EFT) and energy psychology.

Energy psychology works in a similar way to exposure therapy techniques, as it pushes you to face your fear, worry or anxiety and eliminate it by saying it out loud and then tapping on various acupuncture pressure points (it's often called acupuncture without the needles). Bringing your fear into your conscious mind so you can become aware of it would ordinarily trigger a negative emotional response in your brain but the tapping process temporarily deactivates the limbic response, thus disabling the fear, worry or anxiety around the problem. Over time, your mind will start to lose the fear or anxiety around the issue, until eventually you no longer feel any emotional triggers around that problem. This means that you won't be storing any negative emotions that would have resulted from the experience either. EFT (or tapping) is something I use a lot in my life and it is a simple tool that anyone can use.

EXERCISE: Reducing Fears and Worries with EFT

Find a quiet spot to sit. Start by tapping on the spot just above your eyebrow with your index and middle fingers of one or both hands (or use all the fingers to cover a wider space). Still gently tapping, move down to the cheekbone, then down to under the nose, and then onto the chin. Keep tapping gently with your fingers to release any trapped or stuck energy. Move your fingers down to the breastbone, then just under your armpit, and finally, tap on the top of your head.

We can also use EFT to reduce anxiety. Often, we feel stress and anxiety in our chest or around the thymus, so tapping on the breastbone when we are feeling overwhelmed or anxious really helps. It releases any stuck or stagnating energy and gets it moving around your body, a bit like a body decluttering.

The more conscious we are of our thoughts and feelings, the more we start to see patterns. Our minds work in templates and patterns, constantly repeating (and seeing) things. When we pick up a belief (usually in our early years), our mind stores it in our subconscious as a pattern or template. This becomes a neurological pathway which dictates all actions related to that pathway from then on. As you start to see yourself more clearly and become more aware of your actions, you will notice these patterns. By going to the source of these patterns – or the first pathway that was laid down – you can quickly begin making a lot of changes.

There are many tools and techniques to help us recognise these patterns and rewire these beliefs. We can enter the subconscious mind with therapies, journaling, hypnosis, guided meditation and intuitive questioning techniques, or we can go back into the 'past' with transcendental meditation and energetically change our DNA, which then filters down into the future. DNA activations and sound, frequency and light therapies work well too as they can potentially allow us to reactivate 'dormant' DNA in our field as well as energetically change the low-vibrational frequencies in the body.

Remember, the past is just residual, trapped energy stuck in your energy field in the form of an emotion (memory or belief) which can essentially be seen as a frequency (because everything is frequency). I have often found that negative memories that keep popping up in my mind are signs of things I need to work on or still process: messages from my body or the energy field. There are many ways to start the process, but always keep in mind that clearing, healing and releasing trapped energy on a regular basis is the key. Whatever we do makes a difference.

When we release old ways of thinking or limiting beliefs from our mind, we are releasing trapped energy which, for many of us, has been there for decades. This energy can then be used to create a new reality, one where you achieve all that you want and have the life that you have always dreamed of having.[59] While we are working on our limitations and beliefs, we can simultaneously start creating and attracting the life and dreams we really want. The next chapter will dive into how we can use manifestation (or creation) and visualisation to finally create the success we want.

If you are holding yourself back in some way, it's important to work through your limiting blocks, beliefs and patterns to understand why you aren't moving forward. Additionally, keep working on raising your frequency and vibration using your heartfelt feelings. When you consider that we are all connected, you realise that we are all sharing our limitations and beliefs with each other. This is often referred to as the 'collective consciousness'. Freeing yourself from these patterns will change your life and accelerate your success like nothing else you have ever experienced, as well as the people around you.

THREE

Energetically Creating Your Best Life

When I was young, I loved magic. I remember summers pretending to be a witch, creating spells in test tubes and burying them in the garden. This passion for magic led to an early obsession with astrology, which led to a love of tarot cards. All this changed when I had a tarot reading that didn't sit well. The reading said I would only have one baby (a baby boy). I soon discovered that the reading wasn't the problem. The problem was that through the reading, I learned that I had a deep-rooted fear about never having children... in particular, never having a baby girl.

Most people would have just laughed it off and forgotten about it, but because it hit a nerve with me,

I couldn't stop thinking about it. Further readings couldn't eliminate the fear. For years afterwards, I followed a strict fertility diet, significantly reduced my alcohol levels and switched to herbal tea. I became so focused on this that I suspect I created a self-fulfilling prophecy. This was a powerful limiting belief that kept me in its grip for years.

After I finally met my husband and got married at the age of thirty-nine, we first had a miscarriage but after a six-month course of Chinese herbs and acupuncture, we went on to have a healthy baby boy. I was happy, but my old fear had returned. Still wanting to have a baby girl and now being forty-two years of age, I followed the gender diet, used the Chinese gender calendar and bought a bracelet with charms representing my two children – a blue fish and an orange starfish. I looked at it every day, visualising and thinking about my baby girl. Two weeks after I stopped breastfeeding my son, I was pregnant with my daughter.

Although there are other examples from my life I could use, I use this one because it felt like a magical and synchronistic time where my dreams came true regardless of other problems in my life. Of course, I have now explored and journaled on why I wanted a girl so badly and I can see that because I'd had a difficult relationship with my mother, I wanted to have a girl as a way to heal. The tarot reading triggered something inside me that I then needed to work on and energetically clear, but I didn't know about self-sabotage back then, or my inner world. I have always been intuitive, but ignored it. On an energetic level, perhaps our bodies and minds seek out the same experiences as a way of being able to work through the issues that they want to resolve in a bid to release the trapped energy (belief or emotion) around these and free ourselves from the past. This is why I take notice of images and thoughts that pop up in my head now and explore them.

As we discussed in the last chapter, research has shown that consciousness can exist without a physical body in the energy field. If I existed as 'consciousness' in the energy field and sensed that my relations were struggling with low self-esteem, lack of self-belief, depression, misery, pain and a lack of understanding of who they really were and what they were truly capable of, I know that I would want to help them work through this. By freeing myself from the past (although there is always more to do), I have cleared it from my DNA and, by default, freed the DNA of family generations to come.

I learned great lessons from this tarot experience. First, that I am in charge of my life and no one can tell me how it's going to pan out. Second, that I can override any fear, belief or programming through desire, intention and action. Focusing on our true desires in a positive way allows us to stay in a high-vibrational and more conscious state of mind and bypass our subconscious fears and worries. Once I felt genuinely happy instead of desperate, I manifested what my heart wanted above all else. Notice the difference. It wasn't what my *mind* wanted – it was what my *heart* wanted. It was a positive, high-vibrational feeling coming from the heart. This is why 'should' goals often don't work (goals that you think you should have). They come from the mind and not the heart, and although the mind is far from a limited place, there are different aspects of it that can limit us if we don't intentionally know which part we are working with.

Change your life by being intentional

When you set an intention, tell your mind to do something, or command your brain to act in a certain way, it is amazing what you can achieve and how it can help you live a better life. The problem is that most of the time we aren't actively setting intentions.

Setting intentions focuses our energy onto what we want to create, but how often do we sit down, set *one* conscious intention for our day and then follow through on it? Here is a short exercise to help you start setting intentions for the life you want.

EXERCISE: Set Your Daily Intentions

Every morning, after your alarm goes off but while you're still in bed, take a moment for yourself. While you're still comfortable and cosy, keep your eyes

closed and think about how you want your day to
go. Don't worry about your to-do list. Set a positive
intention about what your day will look like, even just
one positive thing. For example: 'Today, I will focus on
doing one money-making activity in my business before
I do anything else.' This can make a huge difference. It
focuses your mind and brings it into reality.

Setting intentions as you wake up is a good discipline
because when you are in a state between sleep and
awake, you are tapping into your theta brainwaves,
which go directly into your subconscious mind. This
is the part that you want to access to make changes,
and the more you do it, the faster you can rewire your
subconscious mind.

Once we set an intention or make a command to our
brains, we switch our minds on. This creates an energetic thought or purpose and harnesses consciousness
so that it can start to create magic in our lives, or 'bring'
us what we desire. We are bombarded by thousands
of bits of information every day, so our brains have
created an alert (arousal) system called the reticular
activating system to focus on what we need to and filter
out what we don't need to.[60] When we set an intention,
this becomes our focus. Our brain starts to look for this
while our energy (consciousness) gravitates towards it,
allowing us to 'observe' what we want.

The observer effect

The observer effect was first discovered during an experiment called the double-slit experiment, which demonstrated 'that little particles of matter have something of a wave about them' and that observing these particles had a dramatic effect on their behaviour.[61] This experiment has since been repeated many times by many different physicists and nearly always shows the same result: we can alter the behaviour of electrons by simply observing them. These electrons can be in hundreds of places at the same time and exist in a field of potential. They only become static and visible when observed.

As Dr Joe Dispenza discusses in his book, *Becoming Supernatural: How Common People Are Doing the Uncommon*, when we 'observe what we want', we energetically create what we want. Taking action on our dreams starts the chain reaction off as our frequency then starts to look for a matching frequency in the energy field.[62] Further research has shown that consciousness pre-empts what the observer is expecting to see, and that atoms behave either like a wave or particle depending on the observer's expectations and thoughts (or even beliefs, as they affect our expectations and thoughts), prompting John Wheeler from Princeton University to change the term 'observer' to 'participator', as we co-create with the subatomic realm (and consciousness) to create our own reality.[63] This means that when we set the intention, consciousness not only knows what

we want, but it then goes about bringing it to us in frequency form, which we collapse into physical form. It
appears to be a massive feedback system that is driven
by our intentions, magnetised by our heart and brought
into form by consciousness.

Using energy to figure out your true intentions

To start homing in on your intentions and understand
what you want, it's important to be acutely aware of
your energy or consciousness, because the clues and answers are all in the energies that you feel inside. Trusting yourself implicitly is essential for connecting to
your inner world. All those subtle energies, vibrations
and intuitive feelings are your energy (or body) trying
to connect with you. As soon as you feel anything at
all, you need to stop and look inwards to understand
what is happening.

Learn to trust yourself and start listening to your inner
voice. If anything feels off or not right, then explore it.
You don't have to do anything you don't want to, but
you should explore your reasons, because you may
be tripping yourself up. This is where your analytical
mind comes in handy. When you feel a subtle feeling
inside, you can question yourself by meditating or
journaling on it to get to the real answers of why you
don't want to do something. If you've got a good reason
for not doing something, then that's fine. If the reason

for not doing something is no longer relevant, you can address it and let it go, making room for change and growth.

You can also practise kinesiology techniques such as muscle testing or the sway test. These allow you to feel what is right (or not) through your body's subtle messages by helping you to connect to the subconscious mind or body.

- The muscle test: Link both your index fingers and thumbs to create a circle. Now ask yourself a question or make a statement such as, 'I have money blocks in my life,' or, 'I am living my life's purpose.' Now try pulling your index fingers apart. Do they pull apart easily or do they stay firmly linked? If they pull apart easily then your statement is false. If it is hard to pull them apart then your statement is true, because the energetic alignment of the 'truth' creates a stronger network and grip. The body, aka the subconscious mind, always knows what is truth.

- The sway test: The sway test is a similar process as above, but instead of using your fingers, you sway back and forth. First, program your subconscious mind by saying, 'Yes, yes, yes,' out loud and feel yourself starting to sway forward. Then say, 'No, no, no,' out loud and feel yourself starting to sway backward. Now make a statement such as, 'I know how to realise my dreams,' and see what your answer is. If your answer is no, your next statement could be, 'I know how to increase profit in my business.' As it all works on one-word answers, ask each question one at a time until you have all the information you need to take your next step.

If you find it hard to do these techniques then try dialling down your analytical mind. You are probably overthinking it or trying to engineer the outcome. Let your consciousness take over, because this is the intelligent, intuitive, knowing part of you.

Because our energy always knows what is and what isn't right for us, we can do these tests with food, people, places and more. Our energy knows when something is not right for us, but how often do we ignore these subtle feelings or hunches and convince ourselves that it's all OK? Our energy knows who we shouldn't be working with and is always trying to tell us. Luckily, the more you work in this 'energetic' way, the stronger your intuition will get and you will know the answer to these sorts of questions immediately. You just have to bypass the ego and listen to the subtle energies of your body.

It was recently discovered that the gut houses around 500 million neurons (brain cells). It has its own brain, so it can make faster 'decisions' for itself and work independently, but it's also continuously connecting with the brain via the vagus nerve.[64] In fact, the gut, heart and the brain (along with other internal organs) are constantly talking to each other and sharing information via the vagus nerve, which not only connects the body to the brain, but when stimulated or activated can also reduce stress, improve resilience and help us to be more intuitive.[65] When we consider that they are all energetically connected – along with every cell, atom and molecule of the body – we can begin to see where these subtle feelings, hunches and intuitive thoughts come from.

Creating a more high-vibrational you

In 1991, Andrew Armour discovered that the heart also has its own brain in the form of approximately 40,000 neurons (brain cells). This 'heart-brain' is constantly sending messages to the brain. It sends significantly more messages to the brain than the other way round and plays a larger role than originally thought. For example, scientists previously believed that pain (which is not only a sensory experience, but also has emotional, cognitive and social components) was always created by the brain, but a 2019 review by A Alshami found that the heart is probably a key moderator of pain. The heart has long been considered the source of emotions, desire, and wisdom.[66] What if the heart is also receiving messages from the energy field and higher consciousness, along with the receivers of the brain, in order to guide the brain, body and mind with the consciousness of the quantum realm?

The HeartMath Institute have been studying the heart for over two decades: heart-brain coherence in particular.[67] The brain has its own electromagnetic energy field, but the heart has one too, and it's far more powerful than the brain's. We can magnify the heart's magnetic energy field, creating a far bigger electromagnetic energy field around us, and fill it with high-vibrational, loving energy and thoughts that attract what we desire back to us. Studies have discovered that when the heart and brain are in a coherent state, the heart, mind and emotions are in energetic alignment with each other.[68] This helps the mind and body to get into an alpha brainwave state (and beyond), helping to tap into a calmer, creative and more intuitive you so that you can access far deeper wisdom and understanding about your business and life.

One of the things people frequently say to me is that they don't know how to be happy or they can't maintain that elevated state of being to start creating a better life for themselves. Creating or manifesting your own reality by harnessing and tapping into your own high-vibrational energy is not about happiness per se (although that does help). We become happy the second we choose to be happy, but staying in a happy state with the stresses and strains of modern living is something we all struggle with. Creating your own reality is more about your state of being than pretending to enjoy every aspect of your life. One way to achieve this state is through prayer. (Prayer is not religion – it's a brainwave state which we will come to later.) Social media is full of people pretending to enjoy their lives, but you can't fool your energy, and it's your energy that creates your life. Frequency and staying in an elevated state of being is what makes the difference. The highest frequencies of all are love and compassion. Not just love of others, but love of yourself, because without love of yourself you will not be able to receive all the abundance and prosperity that you are surrounded by daily.

We are not designed to feel happy all the time but we *are* designed to sit in elevated states of being when we focus on doing so and we *are* designed to live intentionally (consciously) when we focus on doing so. This means we are designed to live the amazing lives that we create. Our minds are incredible and are in charge of it all, except most of us aren't in charge of our minds. For example, something that I found really hard to change in my own thinking was to remember to think about what I wanted. I kept thinking about what I didn't want, but the brain doesn't understand negatives (nos and nots): if you are thinking about it, you will attract it. I had to work hard on this negative thought pattern and discovered it was linked to many other things, which I would never have consciously discovered. No one is perfect and I still have days when I struggle, but then I observe my thoughts, see the truth and realise that it's time to clear my energy field or meditate until I feel better again.

Visualising what you want

Visualising our dreams is important because our minds cannot tell the difference between fact and fiction. When we see something in our minds, our brains believe we are already living in that reality and then start to create the biology around it. Of course, this can work against us in stressful situations, when we use negative self-talk or if we have low self-esteem or low self-confidence, but it can work in our favour if we focus on the reality that we want to experience. By using visualisation to embody or live in the reality of whatever it is we want, our energy is already there. This is also referred to as mental rehearsal or even creation. There is much research which indicates that we can create physical outcomes in our lives by focusing our minds on them and using repetitive actions. Visualisation is a technique used in elite sports and other professional fields. A 2003 study showed that when weight-lifters visualised lifting weights, it triggered similar activity in brain regions to those triggered with a physical performance of the task. The brain responds to a vivid mental image in the same way as to a real experience.[69] This means that the energy field of our mind can affect tangible things (matter) too, which is exactly what quantum physics is showing us to be the case.

EXERCISE: Visualising a New Reality

Find a quiet place to sit. Close your eyes and pull your focus back behind your eyes. Think about what it is that you really want to bring into your life. Feel this desire in your heart, because this is the magnetic charge that will take it out into the quantum field and attract back what you want. Take this opportunity to bypass all the programming from your past and go straight to something that you want more than anything. These can be objects, experiences or desires (such as writing a book). Spend a few minutes every day sitting in meditation and desire, thinking about what you are trying to create while focusing on the joy that these things will bring you.

As it can be hard for some of us to manifest money (if you are not able to receive enough money, there are probably other factors at play), it's easier to think about what you would spend that money on and visualise that instead. Let these feelings of love and high energy envelop your entire being as you feel the pure joy of living your dreams and goals. If you get any inner critical voices saying you can't have it – be aware that you have now found a limiting belief to work on and heal.

Gratitude

Feeling grateful works on two levels. First, when we feel grateful for something (or say thank you), it's usually because we have already received it, so the brain believes we have it. Second, gratitude is a high-frequency feeling to sit in and actually changes our physical and mental state of being. It opens us up inside and allows us to become a vessel channelling high-frequency feelings and helping us to receive more. Feeling grateful helps us to bypass unhelpful pre-programming just as high-vibrational, heartfelt feelings do.

Studies carried out by the HeartMath Institute have shown that we can change the expression of our DNA with our minds (known as the field of epigenetics and discussed in the last chapter). In one experiment, an individual was asked to generate heart coherence (essentially a mixture of heart breathing and positive emotions) and focus their mind on changing the DNA inside three test tubes. The individual was able to intentionally and simultaneously unwind two of the DNA samples to different extents and leave the third unchanged.[70] Control groups with low ratios of heart coherence were unable to alter the DNA in the test tubes. This not only shows how powerful our intentions can be, but the DNA only changed once the participants had felt gratitude for it. If we can change our DNA by feeling grateful, then think what gratitude can do for our own lives or businesses. If you're not already keeping a gratitude journal, you should really think about doing so. Thirty days of daily gratitude will change your life and business so fast it will feel like magic.

Being in a state of receiving is a key part of energetic growth. We can feel as happy as we want to feel, but if our subconscious mind is broadcasting limiting thoughts or beliefs, we can block ourselves to receiving our true dreams or sabotage them when we do receive them. Sitting in gratitude and feeling it from the heart four or five times a day will allow you to bypass your subconscious mind during times like this and start changing your life while working on your beliefs behind the scenes. You don't have to sit in high-frequency feelings every second of the day; even a few minutes will make a difference. It's the regular practice that rewires your brain.

The synchronistic state

Being open to the synchronicities of life is not only one of the most enjoyable things I have ever experienced, but also explains how consciousness works in our favour. We already know that life works better for us when we feel happier and less stressed, but when we start noticing those subtle energies, vibrations and feelings, we can see these patterns on a whole new level. The universe works in fractal patterns and our minds do, too. Once you open your mind and start seeing what's around you and trusting in yourself a bit more, your life will start to unravel in a way that feels amazing.

I once worked with someone who felt stuck in her line of work and didn't really enjoy it, but she didn't know what else she wanted to do. After a session one day, she walked straight out of her house and into one of the most synchronistic moments of her career. She had been doing a lot of inner work, so her dreams were finally starting to break through the filters in her energy field in the form of 'signs'. Still ignoring her heart, and not trusting herself, a few months went by and she received several more signs.

Her overplanning and overthinking nature was causing her confusion about whether this was the right direction for her. She wanted to plan out every last step (with guarantees that it was the right one) before even starting on the first step, but we can only ever know what we fully want in the present moment, because living in the present moment is the only reality we actually have. By focusing too far ahead, we either create stress or impatience for ourselves (which is low-vibrational) or an expectation for things that might not be the right path for us.

These signs may not be taking her in the direction her strategic mind wants to go in, but they are taking her in the direction that her heart wants to go. (If you want to set your goals and then work on making those a reality, this is fine too. It just depends what 'type' of person you are.) Doing it the heart-led way will help you to end up doing something you love and take you to the high-vibrational state of creation, abundance and prosperity.

As well as learning to trust the heart, learning to trust our energy is also crucial, but something that many of us struggle with. Many of us would not accept these 'helping hands' with open arms, because we experience fear when we approach anything new. We often don't believe in signs from the energy field and we still have confusion around whether this is the right step for us. It is our belief systems holding us back.

If your dreams are not manifesting fast enough, it could be for any of these reasons:

- You are not energetically aligned to your dream or goal, which usually means that your heart doesn't want it or it's not aligned with your higher self or soul.

- You are being too vague about what you want and need to be more specific.

- You are accidently broadcasting low-frequency vibrations out of your energy field and may need to look to your emotions, feelings, thoughts or stress levels.

- You are blocking yourself from receiving what you want most through the hidden pre-programming of your subconscious mind (either from this life or past lives) and need to do some journaling to unlock what it may be.

- You are not taking enough heartfelt action to set off the frequency to be realised in the energy field.

- It's not the right thing for you as there is something better coming your way (divine timing).

- You have collective unconscious beliefs or traumas (eg, unworthiness, low self-esteem, fear) that are stuck in your auric field and blocking the flow of more abundance and prosperity into your life.

- You have internal conscious fears (eg, fear of responsibility, fear of success or failure, fear of visibility, fear of rejection) that you are not addressing. Journal or meditate to find out what these are.

When our energy fields are filled with incorrect stories and pre-programming, they reflect as low self-worth, money sabotaging and more, and the better life we are trying to manifest simply can't break through and reach us. This is why it's so important that we work on our own limited thinking to free up space and let the abundance and potential stream through.

Forgiveness

In one of my first podcast episodes, 'Super Energies', I talk about forgiveness being a 'super energy' because it changes our internal state of being in the same way as gratitude does.[71] It not only helps us to release trapped emotions in the form of resentment, regret, bitterness, revenge and more, but it also allows us to receive in that moment. Being able to receive something is just as important as wanting it. Many of us have limiting beliefs around low self-worth or low self-esteem stuck in our collective consciousness, so unless we are self-aware and observe ourselves or journal regularly, we won't even know they are there. You can use the muscle or sway tests to understand where you may have unworthiness issues or feelings of not being good enough and begin journaling on where these feelings or beliefs may come from. Also pay attention to what thoughts pop into your head as they may be signs or guidance pointing you to deeper issues that you have forgotten about. The more you journal and release trapped energy by using energy techniques such as EFT or breathwork, the faster you can begin to uncover more of what's in your subconscious mind or energy field.

Develop patience and enjoy your life

While you are busy creating a new reality, you have to allow it time to develop. If you look carefully, you'll see signs that your hard work is paying off. Remember, most of us won't receive obvious signs of lightning bolts and burning trees. The signs and messages around us will be really subtle, which is why I talked about tapping into the energy field with our awareness in Chapter One. To hear messages or see signs, we need to slow down and listen to our inner world and build up an awareness of what is around us and within us. Quite honestly, we have an entire Piccadilly Circus going on around us, but because we can't see more than 1% of it, we don't know it's there.[72] How many times have you been so busy that you ignored those subtle signs which you are surrounded by every day? Electrical hiccups, mobiles or laptops not working and even plugs blowing are all electromagnetic energy, but we don't think about things in that way. When things happen that would have frustrated you in the past, try to let life unfold a little instead and ask your energy if there is a message hidden in there. If you let the energy field around you help you out, amazing synchronicities can happen every day.

The more you bring your high-vibrational energy back towards you, the more energy you have to create a new reality. The adage, 'The right thing or path is usually staring you straight in the face' applies here. You need to wake up out of your current reality (the life or business that you don't want) and start seeing the new reality already around you. Once you start to create awareness of your new reality and put all your intentions into action, you then need to trust that things are working out in the way that you want them to. More importantly, you must develop some patience around it. It may take a month, six months, a year, or even longer, and largely depends on how much work you do on yourself and how much aligned action you take. Trust that it will all work out in the way that your heart wants it to – because it will – and try and enjoy life a bit more. I'll come back to this again when we look at working your energy in Chapter Seven.

FOUR

The Energy Field and Multiple Dimensions

After my mother died, and for the next year, I kept hearing her voice in my head. I didn't really think much of it and assumed that it was part of the grieving process as I went about my day chatting to her. Then one day my sister came to visit and everything changed. That morning I had half-heartedly asked my mum if she wanted to give my sister a message and the voice in my head had replied loud and clear. As my sister and I sat around having tea and biscuits, I duly passed the message on, but was completely unprepared for the reaction it sparked. It was such a simple message, yet it was unexpectedly profound for her. I was quite taken aback and it made me wonder if perhaps I really had been talking to my mother. As life got busier with children and work, I forgot about talking to my mum and moved on. Then something else brought me right back again. This time it was to do with my own child.

Between the ages of around two and four years, my daughter started to talk about her 'other mummy', who had brown skin and grey hair 'like granny' and lived with her sister. It triggered my jealousy at one point and I asked her if she would like to live with her other mummy, to which she replied, 'No, this mummy,' in a matter-of-fact way. After this, I made sure I never let my own emotions take over again and simply observed her or asked questions that allowed her to talk. Over the course of the next two years, she referred to them several times. I deduced that she had probably lived in India and been poor. They didn't have a car, so she had to walk everywhere and had lived in a sort of wooden hut. I can see that this has had a noticeable effect on her in this lifetime, both in terms of some of her interests and dislikes and some limited beliefs.

Interestingly, at around the same time, she also had an invisible friend with a yellow body and black eyes. She continuously saw things in our flat, especially flying around the ceiling. There was one 'friend' with a blue body she called Blueberry, and another called Ruby, both who used to materialise from bright lights and grow arms and legs until she could eventually 'see' them fully. I probably would have put it down to an overactive imagination (I also had a vivid imagination as a child) if I hadn't had the experience of talking to my mother and it hadn't gone on for so long, but it sparked my curiosity and I began to explore it. She doesn't mention her invisible friend anymore, but I recently asked her if it was still here. The way she looked around the room and up to the ceiling, searching in vain for the familiar yellow body, confirmed to me that this was real to her regardless of what I thought. She replied, 'No, Mummy. Squidgy isn't here anymore, she stayed in our old flat'.

I appreciate that all children have amazing imaginations, but from what I now know about the energy field around us, and indeed imagination, I began to wonder if there was more to this than meets the eye. We have physical bodies, but what if some of the frequencies around us don't? What if they exist solely as energy or frequency? What if we could interact with them? As we discussed earlier, consciousness can exist without a body in the energy field. Nassim Haramein, founder of the Resonance Science Foundation, refers to the energy field as consciousness and believes that it is this giving life to the physical body, not the physical body giving life to our consciousness.[73] Max Planck said the same thing when he said that:

> 'All matter originates and exists only by virtue of a force which brings the particle of an atom to vibration and holds this most minute solar system of the atom together. We must assume behind this force the existence of a conscious and intelligent mind.'[74]

As we learned from Chapter Two, every atom, cell or molecule has an energy field around it, breathing life and information into every fibre of our being. The energy field is alive with different electromagnetic frequencies that we can't see, because as I said earlier, we can only see less than 1% of the light spectrum (known as visible light). We are surrounded by many other waves (frequencies) such as X-rays, infrared waves, radio waves, etc, which we can't see either, but we know are there.[75] As Nassim Haramein says, it is entirely possible that not everything will have evolved into a physical body like we have – some may have an energy field or aura, but not the density of the physical body.[76] If this is the case, then they can live in the same energy field as we live in, but maybe in a different form, dimension or state of being.

While we can't see them, maybe others can; perhaps children in the theta state or more enlightened people, both of whom are naturally vibrating at a higher frequency. Or maybe we can simply pick them up with our own minds – feeling, knowing and sensing them by using our own energetic, or multidimensional, field. To do that, we have to go into our inner world. In Dr Joe Dispenza's book *Becoming Supernatural: How Common People Are Doing the Uncommon*, he refers to workshops where he has been able to measure the increase of energy in the participants' brains as they connect more deeply with the unified field around them, especially when they are experiencing profoundly mystical experiences.[77] Energy carries frequency, and frequency is information, so when we receive more energy into our energy field (or mind), we also receive more information. We are all energetically connected to the energy field around us, it's simply that most of us are not aware of this. We are too connected to our own external physical world and the dramas that keep us plugged into it. Simply closing your eyes changes your reality. The more you explore internally, the more you can learn about and understand your true self.

The pineal gland is a small, pine nut shaped gland located inside the brain, behind the eyes. It stimulates brainwaves through its secretion and conversion of hormones, allowing you to move between beta, alpha, theta and delta brainwave states so you can fall asleep and wake up. We don't really know much about it though, and it's now thought that this gland is responsible for many more things, not least because it's located where the third eye chakra is. Research is beginning to point to us being living, breathing antennae plugged into the energy field and regularly picking up frequencies through our bodily senses and pineal gland, even though most of us aren't aware of it. In 2006, it was discovered that the pineal gland contains millions of minute crystals inside it which, under certain conditions, could possibly act as an antenna tuning into the energy field and frequencies around us.[78] Just like a radio picks up frequencies, so too can our brain via our pineal gland. The mind can then translate it into something we understand. Perhaps this is what our imagination is? Our pineal gland acts as an antenna, picking up these higher frequencies and turning them into our reality. What if some of these frequencies even exist in a different dimension to us and we can't see them in this physical world, but we could see them in another one? When you consider that our eyes pick up an incredibly small range of frequencies compared to other living things, it doesn't sound all that far-fetched.

As we start to raise our own level of consciousness, we also begin to change our perception of reality and, by default, start to see more of the energetic world or different dimensions around us. We already know that our minds alter reality every day and fill in the bits that don't make sense to it – mostly because of our belief systems – so we could be seeing a lot more around us if our minds let us. If we open ourselves up to the possibility that there are frequencies or energies that we can tap into with our own awareness, then we can learn how to harness the information they provide to better ourselves and live a better life. Essentially, we can reach other dimensions by changing our own frequency. Dimensions are not 'places' to go; they are all part of the universe and we have access to all of this 'energetically' now, albeit we may need to learn how to do it.

Multiple dimensions

String theory was discovered in 1968 by two young physicists studying at CERN and is discussed by Michio Kaku, a theoretical physicist and string theory specialist, in his book *Hyperspace: A Scientific Odyssey Through Parallel Universes, Time Warps, and the Tenth Dimension*. While quantum theory allows us to see how matter can be created from the quantum field, it does not account for the existence of gravity. String theory allows us to account for both quantum theory and gravity, as it shows tiny particles (eg, quarks, neutrinos and many more) as vibrating strings which can create all forms of matter as they vibrate and resonate.[79] String theory only works with multiple dimensions though (notably ten), which brings the possibility of alternative dimensions into being. These strings are so small that they can even vibrate between these dimensions, creating matter as they vibrate. Multiple dimensions are thought to be all around us, they are just invisible to the naked eye.[80] Perhaps even we exist in multiple dimensions and are not just limited to this physical reality? Transpersonal psychology already suggests that the mind or psyche is multidimensional and already exists in multiple levels of consciousness.[81]

M-theory, which takes the universe into eleven dimensions, describes a further dimension where membranes exist. This means that although the dimensions in string theory are smaller than our 3D, physical world and are invisible to us, M-theory shows us that there may be dimensions that we could see.[82] Michio Kaku discusses these different dimensions as floating bubbles, where each membrane of the bubble is an entire universe. As these bubbles collide and float, they intertwine, break and reform. One of these bubbles breaking is thought to be what created the Big Bang. Kaku proposes that we exist on a membrane as a 3D reality, but other civilisations could exist in these other dimensions too.[83] Physically, we could reach them through wormholes and portals, but metaphysically or telepathically, we could connect with them now.

Telepathy is how we used to communicate before language was created, and according to new research, is something that we can still do.[84] Who's to say that there aren't other species (physical or non-physical) out in this vast universe (and other universes) using telepathy and trying to connect with us? If they are, then we should be able to pick up on that just by tuning into it like the dial on the radio. We can connect to the consciousness of anyone and everything in the universe by tuning into their unique frequency or consciousness. This is often referred to as channelling, which is a deeper type of meditation whereby you connect to a specific frequency or bandwidth of frequencies to access specific information from that wavelength. It is thought to be a synchronization of frequencies between the channeller and the channellee that allows them to share the same thoughts (frequencies). The clue is finding ways to switch our own frequency on to their frequency by attuning to it first.

The electromagnetic spectrum is divided into several kinds of light waves and our 3D, physical world is contained within the limited field of light that we are able to see. This essentially means that if we get beyond light (or the speed of light) then we may be able to enter into different dimensions. Einstein predicted the 4th dimension, which we have now proven and is known as spacetime, whilst string theory surmises six or seven further dimensions of space that are micro-dimensions and smaller than the atom.[85] Higher dimensions would not only be invisible to us, but they would also have less mass and density than us because they exist in a higher frequency to us and are vibrating faster than we are. As frequency wavelengths slow down, matter starts to form, so our low density 3D, physical world exists at a certain level of frequency or bandwidth while other dimensions would exist at a higher (or perhaps lower) frequency or bandwidth. In Pythagoras' theorem he states that all planets have their own sound bandwidth, ie, frequency.[86] All planets, dimensions, and even humans, have their own unique frequencies. Our range of frequencies allow us to exist within a certain frequency range. Other dimensions have their own too, so by changing our frequency, we can enter into different dimensions. We are probably already doing this; we just don't know we are.

As humans, we have evolved to experience our physical world in only three dimensions (length, width and depth), essentially because we only required 3D vision to be able to spot predators, so our brain is not currently wired or able to 'see' beyond this. This doesn't mean that we can't experience things in our inner or metaphysical world by using our 'antenna' to pick things up. As we discussed in Chapter One, the brain works in frequencies by receiving them and translating them into the physical world that we see. As humans evolve, I'm sure our brains and energy will evolve, too. Indeed, it may already have done for the younger generations. These dimensions may hold the key to phenomena such as the experiences of my daughter or other phenomena in our world. As Nassim Haramein explains in episodes nine and ten of his Quantum Revolution series, what we perceive to be phenomena are not really phenomena; they're just science that we haven't discovered yet.[87]

If you consider the different realities that we currently live in on this planet, you can start to comprehend how our state of being or level of consciousness – whether mental, emotional, physical or spiritual – already provides a completely different reality for all of us, regardless of other dimensions. For example, an entrepreneur who feels they deserve their success is going to see and perceive the world differently to an entrepreneur who doesn't feel good enough because of childhood traumas or subconscious beliefs. Our thoughts, feelings and beliefs lead to actions, which then create our successes. The smallest living organism on earth, the *Nanoarchaeum equitans*,[88] most likely has no recognition of us at all. We are far too big, so it lives in a completely different reality, or even dimension, to us. It may even be able to cross between dimensions that we can't because we are too big. We already know that animals can see more of the visible light spectrum than we can, so what reality are they experiencing that we aren't aware of?

It's the same for us living on this planet: we are a speck of dust in a universe that is full of planets, galaxies, solar systems, black holes, stars, and possible multidimensional realities. If we keep an open mind and stop limiting ourselves, we can start to change our own physical world. If we recognise that we are consciousness experiencing reality inside a physical body (which isn't physical anyway), and that we are simply projecting our likeness onto an electromagnetic field which then reflects back to us what we look like based on DNA which we can change, which in turn creates our own reality – then doesn't life start to look a little better? It does for me. It's thinking like this that expands our mind and stops us from focusing too much on the irrelevant, petty or fearful stuff. Becoming a big thinker – or stretching beyond our current reality – will allow you to step over day-to-day, all-consuming, fearful conversations, arguments and worries and allow you to put it all into perspective.

The world is an amazing place and we literally have creation at our fingertips. You truly can create any reality you want. If I still haven't managed to convince you how amazing you really are yet, then let us look back to the energy field for further guidance and support.

Working with the collective consciousness

Essentially, the more we work on ourselves and raise our own level of consciousness, the more we can tap into these higher frequencies around us, because we are releasing low-vibrational frequencies that are keeping us stuck in a low-vibrational state. As we work on eliminating limited beliefs, we are releasing trapped energy (beliefs and emotions) from our energy field and raising our vibration. The higher frequencies (or consciousness) are the ones you want to tap into as they will help your life to improve and your body to energetically upgrade. The lower frequencies you experience could be yours, or they could be from someone or something else.

Understanding our energetic universe and the collective consciousness in more detail has really helped me rethink certain mental health aspects, probably because this way of living and being has reversed my own mental health issues. Not only has my depression lifted, but I have wondered if perhaps voices that we hear in our heads are not 'madness', but a thought, frequency or consciousness transmitted 'in' from the energy field: a message. The more conscious we are of what we need, the more we can attract the right frequency. Conversely, the less conscious we are of what we need, the more we are exposing our minds to whatever comes in – whether it's helpful to us or not. We attract the frequency we are vibrating at, so if you are vibrating at the frequency of fear or guilt, for example, then this is the frequency you will attract. Certainly, when we consider ourselves as a radio, transmitting and receiving frequency wave-lengths, we begin to understand that we work on an attraction, or resonance, basis.

For example, my husband is Italian and, in my opinion, feels guilty about everything. It's so engrained in his psyche that it's hard for him to see that it's just conditioning. The problem is that this conditioning is stopping him from living a better life. As we said in Chapter Two, when something happens in our life that creates an emotional charge for us, the mind stores it and then omits this frequency (for example, guilt) out of our auric field. We then attract this frequency of guilt, live in a frequency of guilt, and perceive reality in a frequency of guilt. Everything makes my husband feel guilty – even the dog when she's trying to get treats. She can easily see how to manipulate him to get what she wants, as can everyone else. This feel-ing of guilt is controlling his life and also keeping him in a lower-vibrational frequency. To improve his life, he can start being more aware of himself and his thoughts so he can understand when he is operating from his state of guilt. He can also start journaling to understand where this guilt came from – his parents, his environment or even the collective unconscious (as Italy is a Catholic country). The more he starts to create awareness around this guilt and understand where it came from, the more he can begin to remove it from his energetic field and his future.

We understand that these frequencies can debilitate us, but how can we make them work for us? Well, apart from taking a few minutes each day to sit in high-vibrational feelings of love, compassion, gratitude and forgiveness, we can also start to consciously ask for what we need help with. Although our bodies work on a mirroring and attraction basis (we attract the frequency we are vibrating at), it is also possible to connect to the energy field for information, guidance and support. We all have the ability to sense, see or hear energy, but most of us don't know how to as we were never taught.

I find it makes more sense if you imagine the entire universe filled up with pictures (frequencies). This is what frequency or information 'looks' like to our brain or mind's eye, or it translates it into, anyway. It's the same when we hear – we don't actually hear the words that the other person has said to us, the ear takes vibrational information and turns it into electrical information, which the brain then decodes. When we speak, we create a frequency field of information which the brain decodes into words. As we said in Chapter One, the brain is the receiver and translator of all the frequencies around us. Our brain takes a frequency and then goes about translating it into an image, symbol, pattern or even an archetype.

Archetypes

Archetypes have been around for a long time and can be traced back through various ancient texts and mythologies. In the early 1900s, after studying the *I Ching* and using tools such as tarot, astrology and mythology, Carl Jung used these archetypal ideas (or *eidos*) to develop his Jungian archetypal theory and his notions on the collective unconscious, helping modern science to use them as a way of making sense of ourselves and the world around us.[89] His Jungian archetypal theory has been built upon by many, but now that we know about the energy field, maybe these archetypal figures are the energy field connecting with us in the only way it knows how: through the images in our own minds. It is thought that we contain all of the archetypes inside us (in varying degrees), so perhaps the frequencies are connecting with the archetypes (frequencies) inside our own bodies.

What if these archetypes are real or deeper parts of our subconscious mind (and the energies around us) and they come to us when we need their help? For example, the genius mathematician Srinivasa Ramanujan re-created around 4,000 complex mathematical formulas with no formal training. He stated that it was the goddess of Namakkal (known as Lakshmi to many) who helped him and came to him in dreams or daydreams with answers to complex formulas.[90] How did a man from a poor and uneducated background with only one obscure mathematics book to read manage to rewrite not only thousands of complex formulas, but also the celebrated Ramanujan function?[91] Where did this information actually come from, and why did it come to him in the form of an archetype?

Gian Carlo Zazzeri, shaman and meta-physicist, discusses the concept of archetypes being physical entities. These archetypes are frequencies translated by our minds or even something that we have seen before. They may be deeper levels of our own minds trying to make themselves known to us through images and pictures that already mean something to us or coming in from the collective consciousness and the quantum realm. What films or books did you enjoy as a child? Your belief system filters what you see (or don't see) from the energy field, translating what you pick up into things you're more likely to recognise and understand. The problem-solving or analytical brain needs to make sense of things to understand the world around it (although if we get past the analytical mind and the ego, we can step into an unknown world and real potential of the energy field). My daughter's invisible friend probably looked like an emoji to her because she has an emoji cushion that she was given at a young age, so it gave her mind something to hang it on. For someone from England, where Sunday school and church are commonplace, a high-frequency vibration may be interpreted as an angel, whereas someone from Japan or India might see a blue dragon or Shiva instead.[92]

The archetypal images that we see and sense may be different frequencies or other entities that we can't always see with our eyes. Although children and more spiritually enlightened people, who are vibrating at a higher frequency, can possibly see them more as they really are, or how they want to present themselves to us. Maybe archetypes as 'frequency' is the reason why some people feel these frequencies flowing (or channelling) through them so strongly. It is their minds adopting certain traits to help them in life, a connection to a past life (either an actual past life or trapped energy from that life) or the lessons that they need to learn so they can grow. By adopting the characteristics of the archetype, they embody the traits that they or the world needs at that time and become zeitgeists of change, pushing us into a new way of living which, in turn, affects the collective consciousness. Maybe these archetypes come in the thousands to help the world shift? We literally embody that archetypal frequency as it flows and speaks through us, bringing its message to the world. Frequencies speaking and flowing through us all the time would account for those who feel like they have multiple personalities speaking through them continually.

When I look at my children, I have often wondered why only one of them saw things in our home. It has occurred to me that maybe my daughter saw the energies, but my son is more of an 'energy sponge' and absorbs the energies around him. He actually becomes the frequency, which probably explains why he enjoys role play and acting so much. Energy sponges are open to all consciousness and take on the consciousness of others without even knowing they are doing it. Often referred to as empaths, they tend to have more open, energetic boundaries and not only need to learn to set firm boundaries in life, but also need to be far more aware of who they are (and who they are not). They also tend to struggle more with taking charge of their lives (which, by nature, are also low-vibrational); keeping them stuck in a low-vibrational state and more open to attracting other low-vibrational energy into their fields. I was like this. It's probably the reason why I struggled with my own self-identity and happiness for such a long time, but creating a stronger sense of self, firming up your energetic boundaries and being more conscious of your feelings and thoughts can really help. Empaths can struggle more with depression too, so if this sounds like you, know that there are things that you can do that will help because depression is also a low-vibrational state. Dr David Hawkins, author of *Power vs. Force: The Hidden Determinants of Human Behaviour* and *Transcending the Levels of Consciousness* created his level of consciousness chart from over twenty years of research. It demonstrates the range of energetic frequencies on a scale of one to one thousand.[93] Depression and fear are both extremely low on the scale and yet many of us are stuck in this state. Don't despair, you can start the process of rewiring yourself back to a more positive mindset today using active meditations, mantras, affirmations, mindfulness or any of the tools and techniques in this book.

In Caroline Myss' book *Archetypes: A Beginner's Guide to Your Inner-net*, she refers to the archetypes as the way we connect to each other and understand ourselves. She discusses how, amongst the infinite archetypes there are, humanity goes through cycles – some being at the forefront of our society and some becoming less so, depending on what is in our collective consciousness. Myss explains that we live in an archetypal grid where thoughts, feeling, sensations and vibration transmit across this grid, connecting all of us.[94]

In my understanding, this archetypal grid is not only the energy field, but it's an energy field filled with the 'potential and possibility' of archetypes that change with the decades, bringing us signs, messages and wisdom to help us grow individually and collectively. For example, in Marie-Louise von Franz's book *Archetypal Dimensions of the Psyche*, she refers to the 'archaic archetype' that prevails in today's world. She believes it will either end in chaos or unity, and the feminine archetype will keep growing in popularity as we move from a more 'masculine' society into a more 'feminine' one, switching on our innate feminine side for a happier, more intuitive, creative and caring society.[95] We can feel the energy of the feminine flowing through us, and it not only dictates a lot of our actions but also inspires us to connect, share and grow.

Archetypes in today's world are both empowering and enlightening, but as messages around us they can be life-changing because they can help us find wisdom that may have taken us years to find by ourselves. In some of my meditations (and dreams) I have experienced strange but insightful messages that, when explored, have led to synchronicities and coincidences that opened up new ways of thinking, thus raising my awareness and consciousness. These have been hugely beneficial to me, and indeed, helped me write this book.

Carl Jung hypothesised that our minds work in archetypal imagery and symbols. Not only do we see them everywhere, but we can relate most things back to them. We are connected by them to each other all the time.[96] In the foreword of Carl Jung's book, *Four Archetypes*, Sonu Shamdasani describes Jung connecting with mythical archetypes, psychic energies, and the primordial images of the archetypes via what I suspect we would call today channelling or downloading from the energy field.[97] Depending on where your level of consciousness is currently at, it can take time and practice to understand the specific energies channelling 'in' from the energy field. We will look at this in the following chapters, but for now, let's try and connect with the archetypes of your mind and see if you can find some guidance or support. (If you are new to this and want some guidance, then use my free download ruthelisabethhancock.com/book showing some archetypes and try feeling into these images for more information from your mind. Working alongside the talented British artist and illustrator, Tori Dee, we deliberately created colourful and detailed imagery to help activate your intuition so you can connect with deeper parts of you. It's easier this way, because once we have awareness of something, we are now attuned or initiated into that frequency so we can start to attract it.) Everything has a frequency, and as a collective, we are already tuned into some of them. For example, most of us know (or have awareness of) the frequencies of archangel Michael, Merlin the magician (father energy), Mother Earth (mother energy) or even dragon energy from Taoism, although we may call them different names depending on which culture we come from. Others could be Green or White Tara, Isis, Goddess Athena, Shakti, Mary Magdalene, Buddha or Christ. We can connect with them by simply saying the name that we 'collectively' gave them. We call them in, because no consciousness (frequency) can help us without our permission. We need to ask for help.

Think of a specific question that you want to ask or a specific problem that you need help with. This sets the intention, which sets the process of finding the matching frequency. The name of the archetype links us to that frequency.

Remember that we are also simply a collection of different frequencies on an electrical or biological level – it is the software of our mind (the ego) that creates this illusion of self.[98] Even what we call 'self' is either the beliefs of others, our childhood conditioning or the frequencies that we grab hold of (or attract) that come in from the collective consciousness and the quantum realm. In a sense, what we call our self-identity is frequency (information) that continually flows past the neocortex of the brain that we then 'grab' hold of or take on as our own.[99] This is probably why it's so hard to find our self-identity and why we change continually, depending on whoever we are with, what we are doing and what's happening in our lives. It's the ego that creates this illusion of our physical body and sense of self. As we are all one energetic whole, nothing is actually outside of us, although I appreciate that this is hard for us to get our heads around because the ego doesn't want us to. By learning to tap into the right frequencies, we can improve our lives because we are then calling in what we need in a conscious and intentional way.

EXERCISE: Connecting with an Archetype

Find a quiet place to sit down. Relax, take a deep breath and close your eyes as you exhale. Pull your attention to the middle of your head and focus on the space behind your eyes, where the pineal gland (and third eye chakra) is located. Ask your mind to show you the archetype that is most beneficial to you right now. Ask your mind to show you a picture and then feel into the answer. What do you sense or feel is coming through? Try and explore this thought or feeling by asking more questions. Are you sensing an archetype? Which one? Are you sensing or hearing words, or can you see a mind-movie developing in your mind's eye? While not everyone sees images, we do feel or know that they are there.

If nothing comes to you, then try writing down the answer instead. This is by far the easiest way to connect with your inner world and the energy field, so just keep writing until something comes out. Trust that it will and it will. Remember that these are messages for you, and no one else can tell you what they mean. It is your intuition you are tapping into. You must decipher them for yourself. This will probably take time, so it's best if you can find a time to incorporate this daily, eg, at night-time before you go to bed or in the morning before everyone wakes up.

I deliberately didn't include any text to the archetype cards, because they are a way for you to access and feel into your own mind and start getting to know and trust your own deep wisdom and intuitive guidance. I know it's easier (and a lot more fun) to read someone else's descriptions of ourselves, but this exercise is to help you find your own inner compass, creativity, wisdom and truth, which is inside each of us. Ask yourself why you are seeing this image. Ask yourself what the wisdom or teaching is for you. Talk to your subconscious mind or energy and feel into the truth of the answers. Our energy is good at talking to us and is doing so all the time, we just have to get better at hearing or listening to it. If you have someone else's text to read then you may just stop at their opinion or 'downloaded' creativity instead of finding your own truth. Let the universe flow through you and hear the wisdom for yourself. I promise that once you start working in this way you will never look back. It will make you feel empowered and in control of your life and your worries, insecurities and anxieties will fade away as you develop a stronger sense of self, purpose, commitment and confidence.

Our lives will not change until we take full responsibility for them, but we can all be guided by our own intuition and the archetypal entities. Taking charge of your life is an incredibly powerful force, and the second you decide to do it, your energy shifts. It's about believing in yourself, trusting yourself and stepping up or making that commitment to yourself that you will achieve your dreams. Once you decide that nothing is going to stop you (including yourself), you become unstoppable. You and your intentions. Drive your energy.

Archetypal characters

The twelve archetypes Tori painted at ruthelisabethhancock.com/book are modified from Carl Jung's original theory, but archetypes are infinite and can look like anything you have already experienced: animals, people, places, toys, super-heroes or even something from the collective consciousness that you have subconsciously picked up. It's not always the image you see that is the guidance – it's what that image represents to you. Our minds don't talk in words. Their language is the language of symbols and pictures and we have to get better at interpreting what these pictures mean to us. Our minds work in wave frequencies and frequency carries information, which the pineal gland could turn into an image or picture. It could be a true likeness or it could be a metaphor that our subconscious mind is using to bring our awareness to something we need to know. In my opinion, this depends largely on our current level of consciousness.

In Carl Jung's archetypal theory, every archetype has a shadow side. By learning more about both sides of the archetype that we are drawn to, we can uncover limited thinking, self-sabotage and blocks holding us back. For example, the shadow side of the princess is the trickster, the shadow side of the priestess is the witch and the shadow side of the caregiver (or the innocent) is the victim. As Carl Jung says, 'One does not become enlightened by imagining figures of light, but by making the darkness conscious.'[100]

The archetype that comes up could be a frequency that vibrates at the same frequency of a belief or emotion in your auric field (or shadow side) or it could be guidance from the energy field, initiating you into new levels of consciousness and helping you to see and feel more of the energetic universe around you. Feeling into each archetype allows you to start making sense of it all and understand more about what's in your own mind. What is the wisdom trying to convey to you? Try to keep your mind high-vibrational by leading from the heart when you do this or you may get sucked down by the ego again, which is a strong energetic pull that can keep us stuck in low-vibrational thinking for a long time.

More than just the physical

I feel it's fair to say that we have a limited view of the world around us. The reality is, most of us don't get past our own emotions and feelings (that are possibly not even ours), but we are so much more than our emotions and feelings and staying in this reality is vastly limiting our full potential. Don't allow what that person just wrote on Twitter to press your buttons, or get caught up in the negative news the media is feeding you to keep you scared. Step outside of that for a minute and see the world for what it really is. Expand your mind into the realms of fantasy and desire and see which world you genuinely want to live in. Know that you can create this world by working your energy in a way that supports your dreams. You have everything you need at your fingertips, although I know it doesn't feel like that. Please believe me when I say that the answers are not out there: they are inside you. Trust in your energy, trust in your intuition, and trust in your dreams, because this is what your higher self is trying to create for you. Trust your higher self, because it is the true wisdom in you. To hear it, you must let the external go for a bit, which means slowing down and taking a step back.

FIVE

Tapping Into
The Energy Field

We are all part of this universal energy field, filled with infinite frequencies of potential and endless possibilities. Connecting to this deep part of yourself will not only give you more clarity, more focus and more answers, but you will feel more authentic, be able to tap into your true desires in life and be able to find out who you are and what you truly want. There will be no more going around in circles because you have the tools to tap into the deepest part of yourself and discover everything about you. It's a process, not an overnight thing, but you will start to feel more confident in your ability to do it.

One of the most-asked questions I get from people is how to find their life's purpose. Many of us have a desire to make sense of our lives and understand why we are here, and searching for our purpose allows us to do that. Messages from the energy field or your higher mind may be guiding you here to help you onto the path of your life's mission. If you really have no desire to find your purpose, just be guided by what it is you want and don't let others pressure you with their own opinions. Never feel that you 'should' be doing something, because this is the wrong energy; always do what your heart wants as this is your guiding light. Remember to always be conscious of self-sabotaging (and your ego), as this can take all of us by surprise.

As I mentioned in Chapter Two with regards to my higher self or 'consciousness' witnessing my ancestor's struggles, I know that I would feel inspired to 'step' into a physical body to help them. Energetically speaking, I can release their suffering by releasing unhelpful programming from my own body, which then passes onto them. On this basis, if you consider the energetic universe as a whole, it is feasible that the pain and suffering of so many is causing a low-vibrational 'pull' or force that, by default, is bound to affect other parts of the universe. The vibrational harmony is off, and because we are all bound to each other, this is going to affect everything else. We can energetically adjust the vibration of the whole by adjusting our own vibration, because quantum entanglement means we are continuously affecting others with our energy. Every time the body releases some trapped energy (emotion, belief, memories, etc) it increases the level of consciousness.

This increases the vibration of that physical body, until eventually, that physical body is also vibrating at a higher level. If we all do this enough, the vibration of the collective consciousness will eventually shift, which in turn affects the universe. As farfetched as this may sound to some, now that I know what I do about frequency and vibration, it actually makes perfect sense. My perception of reality has changed and I can never go back to the person I was before.

Your purpose could simply be to enjoy your life and work on those hidden stories and saboteurs so that you can become the best version of yourself and reach your true dreams. By default, this raises your own unique electromagnetic frequency. As you raise yours, you will entangle with others around you and lift theirs. More of us living happy and fulfilling lives is what will change the world. If you do feel called to a specific purpose in life then follow your desire, because in your search for purpose you will also find your true self, so it's never wasted time. Follow the breadcrumb trail – it's always there, sometimes we just need to turn our attention to it.

Our language around beliefs and spirituality has changed in the last few decades, and many of us now understand God as an energy source rather than a religion. I have always felt that keeping an open mind is important for our own happiness and personal growth. The universe is a vast place, filled with energy and brought to life by consciousness. At the end of the day, we hardly know anything about the galaxy we live in, let alone the never-ending cosmos that we exist in. For example, the eternal inflation theory proposes that after the Big Bang, space-time expanded at different rates in different places. This leads to the possibility of the existence of multiple universes.[101] What if these multiple or parallel universes are a key to different timelines of past, present and future? Keeping our minds expanded and open makes for an exciting life as we learn more about the universe around us and within us. Nikola Tesla was an open-minded person and saw himself as a 'sensitive' receiver of information, with this information coming from somewhere outside of him. Indeed, he built the electromagnetic motor after the design came to him in a vision during a walk in the park in 1882.[102] There have been many other scientists over the years who have experienced the same thing via dreams and visions. For example, Niels Bohr dreamt he was sat on the sun and the planets were orbiting around him. This led to his understanding of how the atom works and being awarded the Nobel Prize for Physics in 1922.[103] Newton, Jung and Einstein were also said to be mystical in their approach to life. If they had been inflexible people, they may not have achieved even half of what they did. It seems to me that they were all extremely tapped into the energy field or subtle energies around them and used these to achieve great things in their lives.

When I moved abroad and lost my social network and then found myself at home a lot with small children and working online, this ability to connect with feelings or subtle energies inside me not only kept me sane but also helped me bounce back and be more resilient. This was magnified when Covid-19 hit and we went into lockdown. I think we all need to feel supported and loved, because we are a sociable species. Learning that I could feel all of this by going inwards really helped me thrive during this period of isolation. I know I'm not alone in what I felt during that time. Know that you can go inside and connect with your happiness, your soul and even different frequencies for support, answers and guidance any time you need to. These energetic entities could be your mind mirroring what frequency you need at that time in your life, or they could be something else entirely. Either way, this practice can really help you get your mojo and balance back again. Maybe you require a frequency of self-healing, self-love or forgiveness, or maybe it's more information that you need. Whatever it is that you're looking for, going inwards can help you find it. We can even channel these particular frequencies by asking for help or being initiated into that frequency (more about this later).

Journaling for answers

Journaling as a tool is great for getting into the subconscious mind, and journaling after you have come out of a meditative state is incredible. You will often find the answers simply pouring out of you and onto the paper. You can start by asking yourself questions that you want answers to and listen to the answers from your subconscious self. As we discovered in Chapter One, the answers will come to you in a state of awareness and often can't be accessed via your thinking mind. You have to 'feel' them and this is where journaling comes in handy. There are two ways to journal:

1. **Writing to answer specific questions**: As long as you know what question you are asking yourself (or what intention you are setting), your mind will be able to dive down and find the answer to it. If it's hard for you to find the answers, then perhaps doing some research will spark the information already inside your subconscious mind. Another way is to simply keep going deeper into your own mind and the energy field, but you should be prepared to put the work in as it can take time. Often, answers come to me in my dreams or when I am running, watching films, driving or doing the washing up, because these are the times when my mind is relaxed and in a trance-like state. The trance state (theta brainwave) is a meditative state, so it's good for unlocking deep wisdom. Our busy lifestyles are what get in the way of all this inner knowledge and wisdom. Once you realise that it's at your fingertips every second of the day, your entire life will change.

2. **Automatic writing in free-flow**: Writing free-flow can feel amazing. It often feels like energetic healing. In a sense, it is, but there are many other things that can come out as well, from signs and

symbols, to scribble, to actual words and more. Try and be open to whatever comes out, because it is what you require most in that moment. It could simply be a release of energy from your body that you no longer need. Be aware that your ego can still get involved once your mind has attuned to these higher consciousness frequencies, so try and stay heart-focused with your questions and intentions. Feel into it and try and understand what your mind is trying to communicate to you. Our mind, or energy, communicates in metaphors, imagery, symbols and patterns. It's not necessarily what you are seeing that is the solution, it is how you interpret them. If there is doubt as to the meaning, explore it in more detail or ask your energy for more detail so you can make sense of it. Your mind will answer all your questions and your heart or intuition can interpret the meaning for you.

In some of my deeper meditations, I have seen images of things that I have had to think about for a long time before understanding the true meaning. For example, once I saw thousands of bright lights in front of me (you can see the image that I saw on my website, ruthelisabethhancock.com/book). It was a deeply moving experience and I felt strongly connected to these lights. I felt it was my heart or soul showing me that although I may have felt alone and cut off from my family and friends, I wasn't alone. I was surrounded by many others' 'consciousness' vibrating at a similar frequency to me.

Although I have experienced many things during my meditations, one of the most therapeutic was connecting with the consciousness of someone (or deeper aspects of myself) who said he was my son. I tried to keep an open mind as we talked for over half an hour while tears streamed down my face and I felt a huge amount of love fill my body. I asked lots of questions, including why I had reincarnated into this world, and away from him. I received a lot of answers, including why I'm here. Whether this is 'real' or not I don't think matters, because my body still benefitted greatly from this experience. The crying facilitated a massive energy release from my body, leaving me free to let new energy (thus information, opportunities and my dreams) in, while the loving 'higher consciousness' energy flowing through me healed my body and raised my vibration. Once you experience energy flowing through you, it's hard to ignore the truth of it anymore.

If you find journaling for answers difficult, then try writing with your non-dominant hand, as this allows you to bypass your thinking or analytical mind. The more you practise tapping into the energy field, the easier it gets. It's important to also question and double-check your answers as you go along. Examine the information to discover if it's the truth or if you are sabotaging yourself. Never blindly follow anything or anyone; learn to trust your own judgement and intuition about things. Feel into your heart for the truth and trust yourself completely. I promise it gets easier. If you are unsure, you can use the muscle or sway tests from Chapter Three to check what is truth and what is not. You may not know what the truth is, but your energy does and it wants to help you out.

Our own electromagnetic energy field (or aura) has many layers and each layer holds limiting beliefs. The earlier they were set in your life, the deeper the belief is. Often, you can work through one layer only to discover the belief again in the next. It's like a thread woven through it. On a metaphysical level and as a rule of thumb, you can equate every year of your life with a layer of your energy field. As you can imagine, trying to get down to the root cause of issues can sometimes take a while. Learning to tap into deeper and more hidden parts of your mind helps you to find these limiting beliefs faster so you can experience real breakthroughs and transformational moments.

I tend to use journaling, meditating, asking my higher mind questions, or even source energy/consciousness, as my own personal exploration methods. I find after meditating, knowledge pours out of me faster when I write (or record myself speaking) and tapping (EFT) releases trapped energy so I can access more energetic layers on a deeper level. The more energy you release from your body, the more access you have to new information coming in from the energy field and beyond. I encourage you to explore and find what works best for you.

Meditating for breakthroughs

Meditation is an Eastern practice that is thousands of years old and is an amazing tool that can help you achieve amazing things. As I mentioned in Chapter Three, it aids your brain to become more coherent, which helps you to relax and improves your wellbeing. It also gives you the headspace to observe your thoughts without judgement so you can understand them more easily. As we discussed in Chapter Four, it can help you experience astounding insights and visions through our brainwaves and the pineal gland.

Different brainwaves allow us to reach deeper parts of ourselves (and connect to the energy field in a deeper way). To experience phenomena, we need to move to deeper alpha, theta, or even better, gamma or delta brainwave levels. Children are naturally in the theta state between the ages of around two to six years old and then they move into an alpha state (while still dipping into theta) until around eleven to thirteen years old,[104] so perhaps their brains are already tuned into more mystical experiences. Was what my daughter saw real? It was real to her – and that's the point behind experiencing these bizarre images when you meditate at lower (or higher) brainwaves. Our brains are experiencing them, and if our brains are, then we are too. We see the world around us, not from what our eyes see, but from what our brain believes.

Accessing my deep psyche through meditation has helped me find answers to many questions that had eluded me for decades, such as who I really am and why I am here. When I found the ever-evolving answers to these questions, it then became about how I could create a better life (reality) for myself and my family. I also discovered that I could go to even deeper parts of the energy field (or my mind) to access the future I wanted to experience by using shamanic or transcendental practices. We can receive clues from our higher self around better futures that we are not able to access because of preconditioning, fear and incorrect beliefs. Our higher self or consciousness is always trying to get us back to the path that it knows we really want. Our higher self or mind (also referred to as the superconscious mind) can be seen as our inner wisdom, our soul, consciousness or even our intuition. All of these terms are often used interchangeably. (I have added a glossary to my website, ruthelisabethhancock.com/book, to give you my own definitions, but other people may have their own.)

You are always tapped into your higher mind, just as you are always tapped into the energy field, but there are two things getting in the way of you being able to hear it. First is the outside, external world, which is keeping us all busy, stressed and preoccupied. The second is the ego, which gives us our sense of self and separateness. The ego is essential to us living in a physical body, but it's also incredibly clever and ingenious and can come up with all sorts of tricks to keep us where we are instead of where we want to be. Its ultimate goal is to keep us alive – it doesn't care about us thriving. It's the higher or superconscious mind that wants us to thrive. To lose the ego, I find it's best to lead from the heart and soothingly tell the ego to go to sleep. It's still in there, it's just a bit more silent than usual (which is not a bad thing as it's also the inner critic). Meditation is a great way to learn how to tell when it's your ego speaking and how to help it loosen its grip on your life.

From an energetic perspective, there is no past, present or future; everything is happening now. This isn't as mad as it sounds: in reality, your past creates your future in that it creates a belief structure that in turn creates the future that you believe you are going to experience, which you then actually experience. Energetically changing the past changes the future. Why not take advantage of that and remember your past in a way that supports or helps your future – the future that you want to have? At the end of the day, it's just about reaching deeper parts of your mind and talking directly to consciousness to access more information from your multidimensional self.

According to the timeline or 'many worlds' theory first proposed by Hugh Everett in 1954, there are multiple timelines that we can choose to take.[105] These are potential timelines that exist energetically rather than physically. Essentially, every time you take any action in your life, you change your timeline. You can choose the timeline where you don't achieve your dreams or you can choose the timeline where you do. You create your own reality, and you really can have any reality you want as long as you start working your energy in a way that supports that. Magic exists, but magic (or anything else) doesn't happen to you: it happens *with* you. We are all creators of our world and we co-create alongside consciousness and the energy field to make magic happen. Just trust that it is there, because it is. If you are struggling to achieve more success in your life, then there is a useful active meditation you can use for this, where you travel into your (multidimensional) mind and connect with your more successful self.

EXERCISE: Connecting with Your Successful Self

Start by sitting down in a chair or lie down. Close your eyes and visualise pulling energy up from the ground into your body. Feel it run through your body as it passes through your ankles, knees, hips, chest, heart, throat and crown. Now bring your awareness (consciousness) back into the heart space and feel those warm loving feelings spread outside of your body into the room around you. Visualise a golden triangle form around your heart and a silver triangle underneath it so it forms a diamond shape. This is known as the Merkaba; the energy sphere in which everything exists. Feel this Merkaba expand out of your body as it spins and set the intention that you are going forward in time to connect to the more successful you. The you that has achieved the life and success that you truly desire. Feel yourself moving forward, flying through space and time, and set the intention to stop at this time period in the future. When you arrive, step out of the

Merkaba and float down to the ground. What do you see around you? Where are you? Does anything stand out? Notice a building in front of you and visualise yourself walking towards it. What does it look like? Is it large or small? A residence or an office? Walk up to the front door and knock. Who answers it? What do they look like? This is the future you and you can ask them how they got here. What exact steps did they take in order to get to this point. Ask questions to find out what you are doing, what path you took to get there, and what your life looks like in this other reality. Ask as many questions as you need to, and if you don't get an answer on something, rephrase the question until your subconscious mind understands what you need to know.

Meditations like these allow you to transcend limiting beliefs, external chatter and unhelpful programming so you can get back to the part of you that knows what it wants, while connecting to consciousness who wants to bring it to you. These are the multiple timelines that exist in energy form (so are consciousness by default) and we collapse them into the potential of our life.

Now that you know which state to be in to manifest your dreams and live a better life, you can start doing this on a daily basis. Getting into meditation can feel challenging initially, so begin with either active meditations (also known as guided meditation) or meditation music. We don't achieve our long-term 'happy state' from the external environment, we achieve it all from within. You are no longer beholden to others, waiting for them to make you feel good; you can do this all by yourself, right now.

Meditating every day will improve your clarity and focus a thousand times over, so it's worthwhile adding it to your daily routine. Our routines and habits dictate our behaviour and our actions, which then dictate our lives, so I highly recommend trying to incorporate a short meditation routine into your working day. On the plus side, it can also eliminate depression and make you feel more stable in your emotions and feelings. If I miss a day or two, I am OK, but if I miss three or four days, I can start to lose my clarity and focus again. One of the most common reasons that we don't take action is because of confusion around not knowing what action to take (if you're an energy sponge then this may be true for you). Clear the confusion with energy techniques, seal your energetic boundaries (also called Shielding) and use guided meditations to let your intuition or higher mind guide you through.

Downloading creativity and inspiration from the energy field

What is it that you wish to experience in the energy field 'around' you? What do you want from your life? You can create anything you want, and it all starts with opening your mind to it. The energy field is filled with inspiration and infinite possibilities. If you are stressed, pressuring yourself or working so hard that you can't see the wood for the trees anymore, you have lost the awareness of the magic of the energy field. Switching your brainwaves to ones that allow you to be more open to it is crucial, so accessing creativity, ideas and inspiration begins with slowing down and taking a step back. A big step back.

Accessing your brainwaves

Brainwaves were first discovered in the 1920s by Hans Berger when he developed the first electroencephalogram (EEG) that was used in neurosurgery. The EEG picked up waves which he later referred to as alpha and beta (brain) waves in a paper that followed in 1929.[106] Each brainwave emits a frequency which is picked up by the EEG and measured in hertz (Hz). The delta wave is less than 4Hz per second and is the state you are in when you are asleep or in a coma. Theta is between 4–8Hz. This state is how you feel when you are just waking up from sleep or deeply relaxed. Alpha is between 9–13Hz and is when you are relaxed and calm. When you are present with your eyes open, you are in beta, which covers a wide range of frequencies from around 12–36Hz and fits into three levels or states. Low levels are healthy and are learning, report writing, etc. and range from 12–15Hz. Medium levels of beta waves are when you are focused and alert, and signify good stress, for example public speaking, and range from 16–22Hz. High levels, around 22–36Hz, signify bad stress (fight or flight state) which is unhealthy over prolonged periods, and this is where many of us are currently living.[107]

When we slow down and relax, we move into an alpha state with the feel-good, present-moment brainwaves. This in turn opens the 'bridge' between the subconscious and conscious mind so we can access the subconscious in a more intentional way. We can then move into a theta brainwave state, which is a deeper, meditative and healing state. This gives us even more access to our subconscious mind, intuition, the quantum realm and our saboteurs. Once you start to meditate frequently, you can use the theta brainwave state to experience more of the wonders of the energy field and connect to deeper wisdom and self-healing. The next level is the delta brainwave state, which is the sleep state. This is highly restorative and incredibly slow, but it can also be accessed for meditation, especially using binaural beats. You can use the delta state to find deep wisdom about yourself from your dreams. Try this exercise tonight before you fall asleep.

EXERCISE: Asking for Answers in the Dream State

Think of a question and write it down on a piece of paper. Put it next to your bed (or under your pillow) and set the intention that you are going to receive the answer to this question in your dreams. Before you wake up fully the next morning, use the theta state to try and remember your dreams or see if you have

the answer to your question. If you don't, then just go
about your normal daily activities and the answer will
most likely come to you when you least expect it as an
'aha' memory or realisation. If all else fails, then journal
on it. In my experience, it will come out eventually (even
if it takes an hour or more).

Incidentally, if you get a lot of nightmares or don't sleep
well, then try tapping on the breastbone for a couple
of minutes before you go to bed. This will release any
trapped negative emotions or anxiety and you should
sleep far better that night. Anxiety arises from worrying
about things that haven't happened yet, but I also
feel it is a symptom of an overload of low-vibrational
energy too, so clearing it out can make you feel better.
This can just as easily be achieved using EFT as it can
listening to guided meditations that direct the energy
out of your field. If you still get nightmares, then your
mind is probably trying to tell you something, so spend
some time deciphering them. Tap into the intuitive or
'knowing' side of yourself to understand more about
the images you are seeing and practise journaling to
get the truth or wisdom out.

More recently, science has discovered a new range of
brainwave states which nuns and monks have been
accessing for centuries, as Gregg Braden discusses in his
series Missing Links. These are the gamma brainwaves
and are much higher frequencies that we could only
detect with more advanced machinery. Studies carried

out in laboratories using sophisticated scanning equipment, CT scans and MRIs have identified four further brainwave states. These are gamma (36–44Hz), hyper gamma (44–100Hz), lamda (100–200Hz) and epsilon (0–0.5Hz). Gamma waves are thought to be associated with feelings of wellbeing, unity and connectedness. Hyper gamma is said to be the super-learning, processing and memorising state, such as the state needed by top athletes and high-performing people. Both states are anti-depressive and connect us to deep states of intuition and insight. Lamda connects the right and left brain together in a synchronised and self-regulating way thus unifying the brainwaves and harmonising health. Epsilon is so low (0–0.5Hz) that there is little to no neural firing from the brain at all, thus no pulse, breath or heartbeat was detected. However, the monks were still conscious and connected to all parts of their brain in a way that enabled them to do incredible things with their bodies, such as meditate in the snow; the snow even melted around them in circular shapes (possibly from their extended and high-vibrational energy fields), because their bodies were so hot.[108]

When in the higher brainwave states, we are in such a high level of consciousness that we are completely tapped into, or at one with, the energy field, and this benefits us enormously. Psychics and mediums are naturally tapped into the gamma brainwave states when they are experiencing phenomena or connecting with other frequencies from different dimensions[109] and so are shamans (along with theta which is the healing state) when they enter the shamanic state of consciousness for healing.[110] In my opinion, when in this state we are channelling a pure stream of consciousness and because gamma is such a high-vibrational brainwave, we can trust that what we are receiving is beneficial to us.

We can access these different brainwave states by meditating or praying while focusing on feelings of love, gratitude and compassion to all things, including ourselves. We don't have to be Tibetan monks, psychics or shamans; we can all do it as Dr Joe Dispenza has been demonstrating in his workshops around the world.[111] When we are in these states, we are connected to the central energy source of the energy field, which some people refer to as 'source' or 'God' – the highest frequency of all. This is the state where miracles happen, people spontaneously heal and some can even alter the state of their bodies, as in the case of the 'rainbow body' meditations.[112] Our innate ability to do these things has been downplayed by our society through fear and our egos.

Everything in the universe is energy, including us, our dreams, our thoughts, desires and wishes. It's all energy, so it's all frequency or consciousness. It doesn't really matter what you believe; it only matters that you are having a life you enjoy and are achieving what you want in it. Follow your own gut instincts and intuition. Don't follow other people; follow yourself. You are the creator of your universe. You are the creator of your life.

Live your life how you want to live it and be guided by your own heart or that 'knowing' feeling that we tend to ignore. Don't let others sway you or tell you what to do. Make up your own mind about everything *and* everyone.

EXERCISE: Downloading Creative Ideas

To start 'downloading' creativity and ideas, you need to switch to alpha brainwaves and get past the analytical mind, which essentially means 'relax' and let all those thoughts go. Find a comfortable seat, close your eyes and let your mind slow down. Now, pull your focus back behind your eyes and think of the word *creativity*. What comes up for you? Do any ideas or inspirational thoughts pop into your mind? If not, then imagine a dial inside your mind's eye (a bit like the volume dial on the radio in the car) and focus on turning this dial down. Set the intention that this dial is for your analytical mind and notice it going down until it's on zero. Now focus on the word creativity again and feel into what comes up. Incidentally, you can use this meditation to turn down your analytical mind for anything and then turn it back up again at the end. It allows you to access more of your intuitive or creative mind.

This gets a lot easier with practice. Trust that the ideas will come, because they will. You are surrounded by creativity all the time. It's just a matter of accessing it and then deciding what you want to do with all of it. What you use this creativity for is up to you.

What we call left-brain thinkers or right-brain thinkers isn't completely true. After years of studying different brains in MRI scans, studies have shown that there is no anatomical difference between those who are more logical and practical or those who are more creative and dreamy.[113] However, it is true that we process different information in different hemispheres of the neocortex of the brain. Left is logical, rational, methodical and mathematical processing and is where routine is stored, whereas right processes more spatial, nonlinear, abstract and creative thinking and is where new experiences are processed. We learn new information via the right hemisphere of the brain and once it becomes automatic or habitual it goes to the left hemisphere. This is why most of us are left-brain thinkers – we are simply stuck on autopilot.[114]

Doing something new every day will help you to light up your right hemisphere more, and get more creative (even trying out a new café on your lunch break will help you perceive, and therefore experience, reality in a new way). Imagine what travelling, reading, making new connections and facing your fears will do? Every time you do this, you literally create a new version of you, thus catapulting yourself into new paradigms and transforming your life.

We are all creative and intuitive and all analytical and logical, but our education, conditioning and inherited beliefs (what we call personality) lead us in different directions. The more titles you give yourself (or are given), the more limited you will be, but you are a blank canvas. You can be, have or do anything you want. You are the only one holding yourself back. You don't have to accept job titles, family titles or even personality titles, because none of them are the real you. Consciousness is the real you, and although nobody even knows what that really is, it's certainly a far more expanded version of you.

Downloading creativity and inspiration

The energy field is filled with creativity, ideas, thoughts, memories, information, etc. When you create something, you are in a sense downloading inspiration, creativity and ideas (frequencies) from the energy field around you, and your brain then translates it. The brain joins up the dots using your own talents to create a masterpiece. Our consciousness is 'woven' into our minds and we access it as soon as we become aware of it. We then use our genius or talents to translate it into something else. We are all creators and we are creating all the time. If we are not creating, then we often find it hard to feel fulfilled because creating is a key part of what it means to be a human.

If you feel you can't draw, paint, design, write poems or compose music, you are still creative – it's part of your DNA – you just haven't found your medium yet. Alternatively, maybe you can paint or write poetry, but you have never put enough effort into practising it. I was terrible at writing until I started writing every day (as therapy to begin with). Chefs create works of art in the kitchen. Carpenters create masterpieces out of wood. Even mathematicians and scientists regularly find room for creativity in their work. Creativity is, at its root, an expression of your innermost self and your passions and can look like anything you feel inspired to do. Have fun exploring and discovering your unique kind of creativity. Art is about self-expression and can take the form of anything you feel inspired to create. Include writing, speaking, strategising (we are all innate strategists), problem-solving (we are all innate problem-solvers), singing, dancing, sewing, crafting, teaching, etc, into the mix and you will find a medium in there somewhere that resonates with you. Combine your talents with that medium and tap into the energy field for more inspiration and creativity. We can all access the same information from the energy field (and the collective consciousness), so if you don't grab that opportunity then someone else will. It depends what resonates with you and what you want to create.

If there is something that you want to learn or want to be in life, then this may be your path or calling. I have often felt that these callings could be frequencies coming in from the universe that we pick up, like the archetypes acting as zeitgeists of change. Specific thoughts, feelings or ideas resonate with us and we feel them inside ourselves as our own. I feel that writing this book was a cosmic message that I grabbed hold of, messages of 'I need to change the world', 'people should be thriving' or 'it's all about frequency and vibration' rang in my ears constantly and inspired me to start exploring. The way it all fell into place, the dreams and the synchronistic meetings and inspirations, felt quite magical.

Just as we all have our own energy, we also have our own inspiration and need to channel it through ourselves. This means that you shouldn't copy or use other people's ideas because your inspiration flows through you and is meant for you – your higher mind is trying to bring your attention to it. When you feel inspired to do something, this is the energy field speaking through you and now is the time to act. In my mind, channelled frequencies or 'downloads' are the pre-cursor to taking action and I personally don't feel that we are supposed to sit in any 'frequencies' for any length of time. They are messages and our job is to hear the message, take action (or not if it doesn't resonate with you) and move on. This is how I see the human spirit; it's all about change and growth, evolving into an ever-improved version of ourselves. Ever since I was a teenager, I have felt that this was the purpose of our lives: to improve, to reach our full potential and to become better than we were yesterday. Now I can see that raising our vibration is how we get to our full potential and become our innately supernatural or psychic selves. I've worked in people development for decades, but it never occurred to me that this was what the true meaning of human potential meant. I can now see that it's an infinite and multidimensional potential that exists on so many different levels that we do not have the words in this dimension to explain it. We can only feel it.

When you have inspiration flowing through you, you also have positive, high-vibrational energy flowing through you. Jumping on this energy will lead you to the right path, more success, your dreams and everything else you want in your life, as long as you trust it. We often go through our days trying to accomplish our long to-do lists when we are overwhelmed, fed up or exhausted, but you won't be able to download high-vibrational inspiration from this state of being. Inspiration and spirit are flow, and when we are flowing, attracting and gliding through life, we are in the perfect energy for us. Trust this inspiration and use it as the human creator you are.

We are all innate strategists and problem-solvers but most of us are operating from our analytical minds rather than our hearts. I have found that when we access our heart or creative expression and then use our minds and skills to integrate this into our lives and businesses, they start to flow far more easily. I am a keen fan of using all our internal compasses – the mind, body, heart, gut and spirit (energy field) together – to make big decisions in our lives. A good rule of thumb is to follow the exercise above to receive inspiration and then turn that inspiration into your goals for the year. As long as they fit with your overall business or life vision, you can't go wrong. Make sure you are working towards a vision that your heart truly wants and remember that the more expanded your consciousness becomes, the more your vision can shift (or get bigger) so it's worth checking back into it every so often to see if it still resonates.

SIX

Downloading Knowledge And Wisdom From Your Higher Self

We've already spoken quite a bit about the super-conscious or higher mind and how we can relate to and access it. Metaphysically, it can be equated to the 8th chakra, which is located above our head. While yoga philosophy has introduced many people to the seven major chakras that range up and down the centre of the body, from the root chakra at the base of our spine to the crown chakra at the top of our head, metaphysics states that there is an eighth one just above our heads.[115] Metaphysically there are twelve main chakras: seven within the body, four above the body and one below, which are said to energetically connect us to different dimensions.

Metaphysics tells us that the higher mind is like a multidimensional hub attuning us to different frequencies, so in a way, this chakra is like the energetic receiver of frequency, consciousness and thought from the energy field. Our higher mind brings these frequencies 'down' into our physical self as something we can use. The 8th chakra works in harmony with the other three above it, as they are all connected to the energy field and the different dimensions that exist there.

The field of bioenergetic therapies includes healing with the use of frequencies. There are apps available which can feed you a frequency for anything that your body needs (although they generally centre around health and wellness). You can attune or initiate your mind to the frequency that you need or desire by setting the app to the right frequency and then experiencing it. In essence, the higher mind is doing the same thing. Metaphysics states that our higher mind brings the primal code of all frequencies into our bodies so we can then attune (create awareness of) to that frequency or become initiated to it in ways that will help our bodies grow and evolve.

By default, most of us aren't aware of, or don't access, this higher vibrational frequency because we are sitting in the struggle and difficulties of the physical world. We experience the world around us based on what we perceive to be true and what we are feeling or thinking, ie, based on our own electromagnetic frequency. Raising your vibration allows you to access or channel far deeper parts of yourself and the energy field around you in a more positive and supportive way.

We can channel or download this information as words, symbols, sacred geometry, light language, sounds, song, signs, messages and more. The information often comes in snippets, so it can be hard to download entire books or reams of sensical information in a timely fashion (although it's certainly possible, as this is what true automatic writing is). Many writers channel their books, artists channel their paintings and the late Alan Robert Krakower channelled his Human Design methodology.[116]

Reiki was channelled by Dr Mikao Usui in the early 1900s on Mount Kurama, where he fasted and meditated for twenty-one days. On the last day, he had a transforming spiritual experience and downloaded ancient Sanskrit symbols which formed the basis of reiki as we know it today.[117] Reiki is a form of energy healing and practitioners are attuned to the frequency of reiki just as we must attune to other frequencies to experience them. Our brains first need to experience a frequency to then remember or access it again. 'Attuning' can be equated to creating awareness of, or increasing our level of consciousness to, a frequency.

In Ervin Laszlo's book *Science and the Akashic Field: An Integral Theory of Everything*, he refers to the unified field and argues the case for a further field known as the A-Field (Akashic Field) to be recognised.[118] The

Akashic Field, also known as the Akashic Records, is a field of information which holds everything that has ever existed in the universe since 'time' began. As we know from earlier chapters, the entire universe is made up of energy and information (frequency), so in effect the Akashic Field is an energetic record of all this information – experiences, emotions, thoughts, memories or consciousness. Everything that has ever happened leaves an energetic imprint because of the energy that it releases at that time. Laszlo refers to a paper written by Nikola Tesla in 1907 titled 'Man's Greatest Achievement', where Tesla writes that matter turns to matter when cosmic energy acts on it. Cosmic energy is bombarding the planet continuously and, as we already know, energy carries frequency, which is information, so we are continuously being bombarded by information coming in from space.[119]

Accessing the Akashic Field or the Akashic frequency unlocks certain aspects of our psyche, or multidimensional mind, so we can access deeper wisdom and knowledge. How you access these frequencies can be highly personal. Some people use songs and sounds, which are, of course, frequencies. Bioenergetic healing devices can be purchased to 'stream' the frequencies you need to make your life and health work better for you. Words, prayers, music – it's all frequency; tap into which one feels right for you.

I think the reason children love singing and dancing is because they are already connected to the energy field in a high-vibrational way and the theta and alpha state. Once they learn our societal beliefs, they are taken away from that magic and into the sensible and often grey-looking physical world that we have created. It doesn't have to be so grey though. It is my belief that tapping into the energy field in a high-vibrational way allows us to transcend the straightjackets of the current physical world and start creating a better world for ourselves. I suspect our ancestors were far more tapped into the theta brainwave state and so they received much more spiritual and divine intervention or guidance than we do now. These days, we are all too plugged into the beta state and, by default, the external world (with all the distractions in it). We have truly forgotten that the way to succeed and be happy in our life is through our internal selves. The beta state is definitely not disadvantageous to us. It's simply about understanding that we also have other states of being too – ones which can tap us into a living, flowing, multidimensional universe.

How can we, as adults, benefit from being as tapped into the energy field as our children are? If we allowed ourselves to daydream, to sing and dance, to revel in the energy field as they do, how would our lives change for the better? You must empty your mind and go inwards to connect with the energy field and then move your vibration up a notch, to get you into the right state of being or dimension. You can do all this through meditation, play, laughing or just thinking loving and compassionate thoughts until you feel warmer inside. We can experience anything that we want to in the energy field, because it consists of the potential of everything. We observe it into reality with our state of being, intentions and action.

Connecting to deeper wisdom

If you are new to accessing your higher self, then it may be easier to start off with an active or guided meditation so your worries and fears about doing it 'correctly' will subside. Alternatively, you can try the meditation below.

EXERCISE: Accessing Your Higher Self

Close your eyes and focus on the space behind your eyes. Move your focus (awareness) forwards and then upwards. When you start to see a tiny bright white light in your mind's eye, then you are in the right place. That is your higher mind or consciousness – your energy. You can focus on this white light if it helps. If you feel your mind wandering, just pull it back. Breathe deeply, slowly and deliberately and tell the ego to go to sleep in a gentle, soothing way. This may take some time. You should feel as though you are speaking to the deep wisdom and truth of yourself – your higher mind. If you still have that little voice inside filled with negative self-talk or you can't stop worrying about things, then just keep deep breathing and pulling your mind back to the space behind your eyes. Observe these floating thoughts and then let them float away. These are the things you no longer need in this moment. You can let them go. They won't affect things if you believe they won't affect things. Trust in yourself, because we can all do this.

Once you are in a deeper state of meditation, you can start accessing deeper information. As I said before, the success of finding the right answer is all in how you ask the question, or what questions you ask, so trying out different variations of the same question is important too. Here's a list of example questions to start you off, but please feel free to vary them as you go along:

- What do I love doing so much that time stands still for me?

- Am I living my life's purpose?

- What am I too scared to do in public?

- When am I happiest in life?

- When do I feel the most inspired in my life?

- What makes me laugh?

- Is this divine timing or is there something I can do to change things?

- What makes me feel joy when I am doing it?

- If I wasn't in this career, or business, what else would I be doing?

- Do I still want to be doing this job?

- Does my soul feel fulfilled in this lifetime?

- Am I connecting to my soul?

- What is this fear that I am not facing?

- Why do I feel stuck?

- Can I feel the wisdom of my heart?

- What does my higher mind want me to know right now?

- What is my most important business goal?

- What am I trying to achieve with this business?

- Why did I start this business?

- Is this the right business partner for me?

- When did I last feel happy in my business? What was I doing?

- How can I most help humanity at this time?

- Am I playing too small in my business?

- What is my greatest obstacle today?

- What is the most important thing I need to work on today?

- How can I double the money in my business today?

- What is my higher mind learning from this experience?

If the questions are not working, then either try and find a more heartfelt way of asking (because it's the heart that is connected to the subconscious mind via our feelings) or start with broad questions and then drill down, such as, 'Is there something my higher self wants me to know right now? Does it involve relationships, career, love, work, health, family, etc? Is there a better partner out there for me?' I have also discovered that when we ask questions that divert our power away from us and onto someone or something else, we simply get silence, so you probably won't get an answer from your higher mind for questions like, 'Should I leave my partner?' We have to understand that we are in charge of our own lives and will usually not get answers to questions that do not honour this, so if you get silence then try and ask the question in a different way.

In my opinion, when we lead from the heart, we get better answers and more clarity. It also helps us to feel more confident because we can feel 'in the heart' when something is right, which gives us more certainty. Here are some more example questions to help you gain deeper access to your higher wisdom:

- What is the right path for me to take that will make my heart sing?

- What is my next step that will align me with my true purpose in life?

- Which opportunity will make me feel happier?

- What type of work will make me feel more energised?

- How will being more authentic help me to feel happier?

- What is the next step to becoming my authentic self?

- What is stopping me from being more energetically aligned in my business or life?

- What is the next step for me to take in my business right now?

- Am I working with the right clients for me?

- How can I help this world thrive?

- How can I expand my business?

- Who does my heart truly want to work with?

- How can I make a positive difference with my business?

Making a command to your mind is the same as setting an intention and works quite well, but I have found it's better when you attune yourself first through meditating and bringing your frequency up a notch because this connects you to your heart. It's important to understand that we have complete control over our minds and our lives and when we make a command to our brain, we set an intention and start to create a new reality for ourselves. Our minds need us to be specific and intentional: if you are vague then it will take longer and may not even work at all.

Making better decisions

If you are struggling to make a decision in life, try this exercise.

EXERCISE: Making Better Decisions

Close your eyes and focus on the space behind your eyes. Breathe deeply and slowly while thinking about your decision. In your mind's eye create two doors, each a different colour. Each one has a different answer (or possible outcome) to your question. Ask your question and open the first door. What's inside the door? What does it look like? What does it feel like? What do you hear? Is your question answered? Now turn your attention to the second door and ask yourself the same question. What's inside this door? What does it look like? What does it feel like? What is the answer you get? Which one feels better for you? Now, in your mind's eye, create a third door and ask your mind to show you this third outcome. Follow your thoughts or feelings on this one. Does this door feel even better than the other two? Does it feel more expanded, lighter and more energising to you? Finally, look back at the other doors and compare them all in your mind's eye. Which one feels better or resonates with you the most? Which one has better energy or feels like the right path? This is your higher mind, or intuition, connecting with you and this is your answer. (Be sure to feel into your heart to double-check it). Don't overthink it; you may not hear or see anything to begin with, but you will feel or sense something. Follow the feelings that you have inside because this is your energy guiding you to the right decision for you. Your subconscious and body are always talking to you and guiding you, you just need to listen.

Research is starting to show us that intuition can be measured scientifically[120] and by changing our brainwave state to gamma we can even start to access it on demand.[121] The more we can connect to our intuitive self, the more our deep wisdom connects with us. There is no definitive answer on where intuition physically comes from in the body. Some believe that it is the heart (often referred to as the wisdom of the heart) and others believe it is the gut (gut feelings). I believe that it is a multiple approach: mind, body and the energy field (consciousness). As we discussed in Chapter Four, consciousness flows through our bodies, bringing us to life. If we don't let the spiritual in, we will probably feel incomplete in some way.

Your vision

Although I firmly believe that we all have a vision for our lives and businesses, most of us are either not living it, are working towards the wrong one (because of conditioning) or not even aware of it. Once we know what our true vision is, life not only starts to make more sense, but we begin to achieve our dreams faster; both on a conscious and unconscious level. As Paulo Coelho explains in his globally acclaimed book *The Alchemist*, once we know where we are heading and what our dreams are, the universe (or consciousness) starts to align itself towards us.[122]

If you are struggling to find the answers to your own vision, then try one of the two exercises below for even deeper wisdom. The first one is to connect to your intuition and the second one is to 'download' information from the energy field so that you are asking for the information to 'come' to you in order to be realised and then actualised. You can also swap the word 'vision' for 'purpose' if you prefer but I don't advise getting hung up on trying to find that often illusive purpose if it's really not coming to you. Focusing on your vision instead allows you to focus on creation, the future and what you want your life to be about while discovering your purpose (or the meaning of your life) at the same time. I suspect that we aren't born knowing what our purpose is because we need to live our lives first. We have to find it for ourselves. My purpose has definitely evolved over the years, but it has always had a running theme through it and that's simply to help people live better lives. It took me a long time to understand how my soul wanted to achieve this, but as I look back, I can see it has always been there. I just wasn't paying attention.

EXERCISE: Using Intuition to Discover Your Vision

Find a quiet spot to sit down and relax. Close your eyes and take five deep breaths, connecting yourself to the energy field. Focus on raising your frequency by filling up your heart with love and compassion towards yourself and the world around you. Now say the following to yourself: *I set the intention for my brain to open my crown chakra and connect with my higher mind to understand what my life/business vision is.*

EXERCISE: Downloading Knowledge to Discover Your Vision

Begin your session as above. Once you are connected to the energy field, say this to yourself: *I set the intention for my brain to open my crown chakra and download the knowledge of what my life/business vision is.*

Once you have 'downloaded' the information from your higher mind, then do some journaling or automatic writing on the following questions:

- What is my life vision?

- What does my soul desire?

- What am I so passionate about that I would lay down my life for?

- What do I love doing so much it feels like fun to me?

- What is my life's purpose or what am I here to do?

- What could I talk about for hours without getting bored?

- Who do I want to help or serve in this life?

- What do I want to leave as my legacy?

- What am I thinking or talking about when I feel a fire in my belly?

- What do I love doing above all else?

- What am I talking about when I feel with all my being that this is who I am?

- What are my life dreams?

- Am I living my life vision now? (If not, why not?)

- What does my soul want to create in this life?

- Where do I want to be in 5, 10, 20 or 50 years time?

- How does the divine want to create (or express) through me?

- How do I want to make a global impact in this world?

If you are struggling to connect or receive answers, remember that we connect best to our inner world, higher self and the energy field through our heart, so ask more heartfelt questions that come from your own emotions and desires. Even changing the question by one word can make a huge difference to the answers you get, so keep repeating the question, but change the wording slightly until you get something coming out. As always, journal on the question if you find this hard to do.

The five pillars of vibration

Another way to think about your life vision is to think about the five pillars of your life: mental, spiritual, physical, emotional and environmental. We need to be constantly aware of what vibrational frequency (or 'energetic aspect') each one is sending out. These frequencies come from your conscious feelings and thoughts or from your subconscious beliefs and memories (so we won't necessarily be aware of them). Ingrid Sprake, reiki master, explains that as we are made up of vibrating particles, disease, problems, lack of abundance and general malaise are related to an imbalance in a corresponding pillar.[123] These can be expressed via our emotions, mind or soul or be affected by our environment, but to get ourselves back to balanced and happy again, it's important to release or heal the blockages by changing the environment of the cell. For example, in my opinion, low levels of spiritual well-being are where much of our depression comes from. With the rise of the online world, and especially during COVID-19, more of us have become unbalanced in our environmental pillar as we spend more time tied to our computers and less time with our family and friends. If you are dissatisfied with your business or career, then your mental and emotional pillars will probably be affected and will be sending out a vibrational frequency that is unaligned to what you want. Reiki is now listed on the NHS in the UK, so it's a fast-growing area providing health benefits to people everywhere.

In life coaching these sorts of areas are looked at to help people enjoy their lives more, but in energy healing we also look closely at the vibrational frequency of that field (your own energy or biofield) and chakras. Everything has an energetic blueprint – even your business – and it all needs exploring to understand blockages, stagnation, disharmony, etc, in more detail. If your life or business is not what you want it to be, then your vibration is possibly off and it needs addressing or re-aligning. This can also be done through reiki, qigong, tai chi, theta healing, crystal healing, shamanism, reflexology, acupuncture, acupressure, Alexander Technique and bioenergetic healing, as well as the methods we have used in this book such as being more conscious of the frequency you are broadcasting now with your emotions and feelings and working on trapped, stagnating energy with journaling and energy healing.

Everything makes a difference. You also need to keep doing it, because even if you have cleared much of your ancestral or childhood baggage, you're still picking up low-vibrational energy as you go through life. It's around us all the time, in the collective consciousness, but as soon as you have cleared all of that frequency from your field, you will stop attracting it. I say 'all' because each belief probably has many different sub-frequencies under that umbrella heading, especially bigger topics such as low self-esteem, which can extend into lack of confidence, low self-love, not feeling good enough, imposter syndrome and more. Combining these frequencies (beliefs) with all the different areas in your life creates an even larger frequency bandwidth. There will always be more than one aspect or frequency, so it's important to get down to the core belief and release that one. If you keep attracting the same situations this indicates that you still have that frequency/belief, so your subconscious mind is likely hanging onto it for a reason. Keep journaling and connecting with your higher mind to find the reasoning and release it, while reframing it for your subconscious mind, so it can be let go. The more self-development or inner work we do, the higher our frequency will go, and eventually even stubborn belief structures will simply not be able to exist in your frequency range. You have now increased your overall frequency to a level whereby these other frequencies are simply too low a vibration to exist in your field.

According to metaphysics, we all leave an energetic imprint everywhere we go. When you get up from your chair, you leave an energetic imprint – your thoughts, feelings, beliefs, emotions, etc (thoughts and emotions are also energy, so they are included). These imprints can hang around for a while, building up or attracting more of the same frequencies to them[124] resulting in egregores or energy pendulums (which I will come to later) which is why it's important to clear our space, house and workspace on a regular basis. When you are entangling with others, you could be picking up, and taking on, their 'stuff' too.

Our business is the same – it changes constantly, so it's important to review it, check in with it and clear out old thinking, out-of-date clients, resentments and past hurts. These thoughts and feelings can build up over time and create low-vibrational forces, resistance and thought forms or egregores that you won't be aware of on a conscious level, but can really affect your success on an energetic level.

Energetic healing for greater success

Working with energy as a healing modality is amazing. We can channel the power of high-vibrational, loving energy from the energy field and use it to heal ourselves, animals, people and even our bank balance. If you can imagine it, you can heal it.

We can channel energetic healing just as Dr Mikao Usui channelled reiki, but in the same way that reiki students need to be attuned, we need to be attuned, initiated or activated, into specific energies. Dr Usui dedicated his whole life to teaching and practising reiki. He discovered it by reading and studying many ancient

texts and when he was ready, he fasted and meditated for twenty-one days before he was finally able
to access and channel the reiki frequency.[125] You can
start with channelling other frequencies that we have
already collectively named, such as Mary Magdalene,
Green Tara, Jesus, Krishna, Christ, Buddha, Kali or
even source energy (the highest frequency of all), often
referred to as God.

If you are new to this, you can tap into source or cosmic
energy, earth energy, an archetype, the frequency of
healing or whatever you want to call it – it's up to you.
As long as you can feel the pulsating, warm feeling flowing through your hands, you know that it is working.
Calling on the frequency of source energy works well,
because consciousness has an intelligence and seems
to know who or what it is, even if we don't. Higher
consciousness frequencies, which we often refer to as
entities (or deeper parts of us), work well too, especially
archangel Michael, which is a powerful frequency good
for healing your body and eliminating things from
your life, such as addictions. Using mantras can help
the mind to focus and transcend. Ascended masters
such as White Tara from Tibet help us with longevity
and wellbeing. Call on her by using her mantra in your
meditation: 'Om Tare Tuttare Ture Mama Ayuh Punya
Jñana Pustim Kuru Svaha.' (Translation: 'I prostrate to
Tara the liberator, mother of all the victorious ones, for
long life, merit and wisdom.') This is one of the most
significant and most commonly chanted mantras in
Tibetan Buddhism.[126]

If talking about angels and ascended masters triggers you, appreciate that this is simply energy or higher consciousness and a way to channel healing energy, and thus information, through your body. As a species, we have created these collective archetypes ourselves and, as such, they now exist in our collective consciousness. They are different frequencies and don't have physical bodies. They are not things, they are states of being, which we tap into through our intentions and our own levels of consciousness. We live in an energetic universe and tapping into these frequencies can change your life.

Sound is energy healing, too. Words are energy, feelings are energy and thoughts are energy, so use yours in a healing and powerful way to heal whatever you want to heal. We all have healing hands (and intentional minds). We are all 'healers' and there are many ways that we can heal ourselves and others around us. My son has a sensory processing disorder and massaging his arms and back often helps him to calm down. It feels to me like he gets a huge build-up of dense energy and his energy field simply can't take any more. By massaging his body, I can release any stagnation or denseness and help to reduce the overwhelm (and anxiety) for him, as well as set energetic boundaries (shields) around his body. Understanding that the human body stretches out much further than our physical selves helps me to explore more than just the part we can see and this has been life-changing for me and my family.

There have been many studies since the emergence of energy healing. One study recorded pulsating energy waves coming out of the healers' hands as they were healing at the alpha and theta hertz levels.[127] The field known as entrainment was first developed in the 17th century by Christiaan Huygens in his study of clocks. He showed that when two oscillating bodies are near each another, they can synchronise and begin oscillating in harmony, often with the vibrations adjusting to the higher vibration until they are both vibrating at the higher vibrational frequency.[128] Everyday examples of this are within rhythmic beats in music, which is how binaural beats work – they allow our bodies to vibrate at a certain vibration, thus helping us to get into that 'self-healing' frequency and improve our wellbeing and wellness. We can also listen to different frequencies to heal our bodies or connect to the energy field in a deeper way. For example Solfeggio frequencies, which date back to the sixth century, are said to heal the body, release negativity and raise the vibration, as well as help us to connect to the energy field and higher consciousness.[129]

When we truly understand that everything is frequency, it really opens a whole new world of healing. Andy Hill, a professional frequency healer, says that using frequency (information) as a healing modality is the perfect way of improving our health. For example, imprinting water with various frequencies can trigger your body's energetic field, because bioenergetics is a form of homeopathy which has been used for millennia, and revolves around sound and energy waves.[130] Be it the frequency of vitamin C or even the frequency of an apple, we can give the body exactly what it needs in its purest form. We all vibrate at unique frequencies, so what works for one person may not work for someone else. That's why bioenergetic machines are a valuable tool in understanding what frequencies your body resonates at and what's missing.[131]

Raising the vibration (frequency range) of the body can help create balance. This balance is key for the elimination of diseases, parasites and toxins. Your body uses dis-ease to communicate so without creating energetic balance you will never truly heal.[132] Epi-genetics is the study of how your environment affects your internal balance, and as electromagnetic beings, our surroundings make a massive difference to our health. Radio waves, Wi-Fi, fluorescent lighting and even which direction we face in our sleep all make a difference: sleeping facing north is polarised to the flow of energy as our body's magnetic field interferes with the earth's magnetic field, so changing to a west-east or east-west flow can help us sleep better. Andy goes on to say that we know we are guinea pigs to new energy waves and technology, but even making a few simple tweaks in your life can make massive differences to your health. Try the following yourself and see if you notice a difference: put a blue-light filter on all your screens, drink more high-quality, filtered water (water acts as a conduit for information through your body, so confusion and lack of mental clarity could be dehydration) and take all screens and electrical devices out of your bedroom when you sleep.[133]

EXERCISE: 'White Light' Body Energy Healing

There are many different ways to access energy healing, but one of the easiest and most common exercises is a variation on the 'white light' exercise.

Find a comfortable position, either seated or laying down (you may be here for a while). Close your eyes and take five deep breaths. If you find that your mind is still racing, continue with the deep breathing until your mind clears. When you feel yourself settle in, bring your focus to your hands. Imagine them glowing with a warm, soft, white light. Even though you can see the outline of your palm and fingers, the light radiates off them. Place the palm of one hand on your heart and the palm of the other hand on your abdomen. Now visualise the white light from your palms sinking into your heart and abdomen. You may feel a warming sensation, a tingling sensation or nothing at all. Whatever you feel, it is exactly right for you in this moment. The white light may stay where it is or it may travel up and down your body. Continue to breathe and visualise the white light until you feel it naturally fading. Continue to breathe and stay in your comfortable position for as long as you wish. You may fall asleep; that's OK, too. Sleep is the ultimate healer.

When you feel ready to come out of your healing, be gentle with yourself. You may want to journal about your experience, or simply relish the feeling of being relaxed and healed for as long as possible.

Everything is energy – even money – and many of the blockages outside of the body are resistance or a build-up of low-vibrational energy or density that starts with us and our limited beliefs or thinking about things. In the same way that feng shui works to clear blockages in your energy space, so too can any form of energy work.

EXERCISE: 'White Light' Financial Energy Healing

This is another variation on the 'white light' exercise, but instead of healing your body you're going to be healing your finances, cashflow or bank balance.

As before, find a comfortable position, either seated or lying down. Close your eyes and take five deep breaths. If you find that your mind is still racing, continue with the deep breathing until your mind clears.

When you feel yourself settle in, bring your focus to your hands. Imagine them glowing with a warm, soft, white light, and hold them opposite each other. Observe this ball of light spinning in between your hands and set the intention that it will be used to clear or heal any resistance in your energy field and the energy field of your finances, cashflow or bank balance. Watch this light start to clear away any stagnation, and the more you can visualise it, the faster it will work (you will probably need to repeat this if you are new to inner work and healing). I have often found that holding your hands over your 1st chakra (front and back) and healing this area works well for clearing money blocks, because this is related to survival stories of poverty, famine and shelter, but do whatever you feel called to do. Any of the first three chakras in the body can have blockages related to money, because they are the physical world chakras and connect you to this dimension. You can also use the reiki energy to heal the first three chakras in your daily practice too.

Now take this up a notch and feel into your mind, asking for guidance on what the resistance may be. It may be coming from you in the form of a limiting belief or some ancestral trauma, or it may be coming from someone in your immediate network (maybe unconscious fears from a loved one or even jealousy from a friend). Just feel into yourself and see what thoughts pop up. You may see visions in your mind's eye, hear or sense words or just know that something feels right. If nothing comes at all, then finish off the money healing by feeling gratitude and then come out of meditation and start journaling. In my experience, the answers always come pouring out when we journal and you will definitely experience some form of therapeutic streaming of words and thoughts by doing this. Even if it's unconscious and you aren't aware of it, it's still working.

We understand from studies that we do not heal other people. Their bodies heal themselves – we facilitate the brainwaves or energies to sync up so their energy can become more coherent and they can get into the healing brainwave states. Our bodies are good at healing themselves (via the subconscious mind) especially through intention, channelled energies and therapeutic brainwave states and we should learn to trust ourselves and trust in the higher consciousness energies of the energy field.

More physical energetic practices include deep tissue massage, yoga and even sports or jogging. Metaphysics tells us that disease is trapped energy in the form of trapped negative emotions, so any form of movement (and focused breathing) can help release it from our field. In the animal kingdom, animals that have experienced trauma (eg, the South African springbok) literally shake it off their bodies, thereby releasing it from their energetic field. Humans don't have this ability, so we store it in the body or energy field instead. Unfortunately, this unreleased trauma can sometimes end up making us sick as it builds up in the body, eventually turning into diseased matter (waves and particles are interchangeable on the quantum level).[134]

With journaling and EFT, we can also heal our mind and our limiting beliefs, because energetic healing is all about shifting our consciousness or trapped emotions/energy from our field. The power of your mind is incredible and my hope is that by the time you have read this book, you will feel that deep inside you, too. Remember, mind over matter doesn't mean push. Manifestation is not push; it is pull. Flow is not push; it is pull. Pulling energy from the energy field, channelling or downloading information, wisdom and creativity is flow, and because of the different quantum fields that carry energy – including that of the mind – we need to be in flow with the energy field all the time.

SEVEN
Creating More Space

W e are surrounded by abundance (the energy field) all the time, but most of us aren't living abundant lives because we are not managing our energy properly and letting the abundance in. Instead, we are blocking it with our limited thinking, beliefs, incorrect stories and preconceived ideas or perceptions about life. Our energy field is like a projected filter and it's like we are walking about in an abundant world filled with prosperity and dreams, but we only see the black and grey puddles on the floor. Raising our vibration allows us to see more of the colour in the world (literally), as it increases our awareness and allows us to see more of the energetic field around us. Our reality changes every time we shift our perspective.

The more we release trapped energy, the more space we have for abundance. Essentially, the more we let go of old habits and ways of thinking, the more space we create to let in the new reality we want. If all our energy is taken up thinking about the past, stewing over arguments or getting annoyed by frustrating people, we don't have any space in our energy field to let in new experiences. If you are busy manifesting but it's not working, then this may be why. It's incredibly hard to let the frustrations and annoyances of life go. There is a reason why so many negative posts or comments go viral online: negativity, anger and judgement sell. Most of the modern world is vibrating at these lower frequencies, so we see them and attract them back to us. I used to get so triggered by people on social media when I was sitting in fear, judgement, anger, exhaustion and depression. Now I have a completely different experience with it, not to mention I can see the real reasons why people write or act in a certain way. This understanding, combined with working through my own 'stuff' has allowed me to develop far greater compassion – which is one of the highest vibrational frequencies we can be in. The longer you can stay in the frequencies of love and compassion, the better your life, and business, will be.

I am not talking about emotions here (these come and go) – I am referring to your state of being or level of consciousness. I still get triggered by people and I still snap at my husband, the difference is that I can't hide from the deep truth of myself anymore because it's staring me straight in the face. I know if it's self-sabotaging, limiting beliefs, negative thinking, my inner critic or pre-programming driving my behaviour because I can see it and hear it in my own mind. I've also learned that social media can be used in an inspirational way. For example, I only post when I feel inspired to create something or when it's coming from the heart. Doing this helps your energy send love and compassion into the world, which you then attract back to you. Once you start vibrating at a higher vibration yourself, you will stop attracting people with lower vibrations. We are all at different points on our own journey and there is no judgement, but it's important to preserve your own energy and not give it away to others.

According to Vadim Zeland's theory of Reality Transurfing®, we can get stuck in energy pendulums which are virtually impossible to get out of. Social media can be an energy pendulum that you can get stuck in (as can religion, class, hierarchies, cultures, politics, race, etc.)[135] People not only get stuck, they start to lose their sense of self and begin to morph into each other, fuelling the pendulum with reaffirmations and judgements. When we follow other people's ways of doing things, we are, in effect, diluting our own unique frequency or energetic signature. We literally give away our power to the other person and start to vibrate or 'oscillate' at their frequency. It's important to tap into your own wisdom and creativity and your own unique soul frequency (your authentic self) so you can start attracting more authentic people. Start by changing what you read and watch, but most of all, meditate and journal to understand who the authentic person inside you is.

When you are trapped inside a pendulum, also known as an egregore, you aren't able to see the real you. I suspect this is why unplugging from social media can be so freeing, healing and enlightening – you start to get the real you back again. Use your energy to create a better and more enjoyable life for yourself. Don't just give your energy away to others. Feel into your energy or heart to understand what reality you really want to be living in and spend five minutes a day visualising it (while feeling gratitude for having received it already).

Working energy

How your body 'works' its energy is important. Not knowing this held me back for years and I struggled both with my business and getting what I wanted in life. Self-sabotaging aside, I now realise that I wasn't working in harmony with my energy. Learning this set me free and allowed me to enjoy my business and life far more. When we feel struggle in our lives, we create more struggle. When we live our lives from a place of frustration, we send out frustration. When we build relationships from a place of fear or desperation, we send out fear and desperation. I think we all want to attract high-vibrational people and opportunities into our lives, but many of us don't know how.

When we are working our energy in a way that is right for us, our energy flows. Alan Robert Krakower's (Ra

Uru Hu) Human Design system[136] sums this up best. It talks about managing your energy in a way that makes your life work for you. People need to focus their energy on living life, creating and doing their thing while allowing opportunities to naturally present themselves through attraction. The system tells us not to 'push' our goals forward, because this results in frustration (negative energy), impatience and feelings of being stuck when things don't work to our timetable. We should instead focus on what is coming into our life, assess whether it feels right for us, and then work with it if it does. This isn't about being passive – far from it – it's about being in flow and trusting your intuition and the energy field around you to help you create the life that you truly want. When we work with the creativity, wisdom and inspiration that surrounds us, daily life feels truly magical and far more aligned with our soul.

The cycle of flow

We live in a cycle of attraction and flow, so getting your energy into a state of flow is key. When you push life to work to your timescale, you are attempting to 'push' energy. This causes many problems, including not getting what you want fast enough. We can't push energy; we can only let it flow. I used to be an overthinker, but I learned that this is not sustainable (and it's definitely not enjoyable). I used to measure my success based on my financial earnings, but these days I measure

Depletes your energy	Replenishes your energy
Criticising	Love
Judging	Compassion
Moaning	Kindness
Gossiping	Self-care
Feeling unfulfilled	Love of self
Stress	Appreciation
Resentment	Taking responsibility
Depression	Being authentic
Apathy	Genuine
Frustrations	Honest
Annoyance	Doing what you love
Denial of self	Trusting yourself
Ignoring your truth	Meditation
Over worrying	Leading from the heart
Blaming others	Open-minded
Bitterness	Self awareness
Regret	Doing things for the right reasons
Revenge	Forgiving yourself
Fear	Prioritising yourself
Closed mind	Taking breaks
Over-thinking	Enjoying life

my success based on my levels of abundance (ie, how happy I feel or how well my life is going) and simply track my finances instead. Tracking your finances allows you to be fully aware of them (switching on your reticular activating system), yet not obsessing about them. It also allows you to work with your energy rather than against it. When we work with our energy, we create more of it; when we work against it, we deplete it. This depletes our energy field and leaves us feeling drained, unhappy and unsatisfied. The table that follows outlines this concept.

When you begin to work with your energy instead of against it (which is what most of us are currently doing), life gets better and things shift. This can be a difficult concept to master and can be explained in more detail using the 'having versus wanting' analogy (or 'lack versus abundance' analogy).

Having versus wanting energy

'Having versus wanting' energy is essentially about tenses – past versus present – and we must always be in the present. The past is gone and the future hasn't happened yet. If you are in want of something, this tells your mind that you don't have it and you feel lack from not having it. However, our minds only work in the now. We must feel like we have everything that we want already. This is also called embodiment. If we already 'have' it, then our mind believes we already have it and is busy creating all the biology around it. This is what the art of visualisation is: believing that you already have it. The power of visualisation is astounding. You now live in that reality of having it and your mind is tuned into it. If you are stuck in the reality of wanting it, then your mind is also wanting it. Believe it is yours, believe that you already have it and you will. It's so simple, but then flow is simple, too.

Flow means no effort whatsoever, but most of us have different definitions and perceptions of what 'effort' means. What does effort mean to you? Does it mean:

- That you have to work 24/7, drink endless cups of caffeine to keep yourself going and putting off taking a break until you have done that 'one last thing'?

- That you need to work at night or over the weekends on a project or assignment that you can't delegate to anyone else?

- Justification? (That if you simply work harder and harder that you will get rewarded.)

- Putting everyone else's needs before your own?

- Saying yes to requests for your time and energy when you'd rather say no?

Effort doesn't mean any of those things to me anymore, but I used to believe all of them. These days, I talk about flow, not effort, and flow means being energetically aligned with whatever I am doing. It means I enjoy what I am doing, and if I'm not, then I look at how I can change things so I am. This is why I am such a big fan of outsourcing – it's such a win/win situation and creates good energy. There will always be someone out there who loves doing what you hate (make sure you don't outsource things to someone that hates doing it, too) and facilitating an experience where you make two people happy creates a lot of good vibes in your business.

The second you feel effort (or impatience, pressure, stress or resentment), it's important to take a step back, because this means your energy has changed and you are now in the wrong state for abundance and prosperity. The easiest way to break this feeling is to laugh, sing or do something that makes you feel happy. This will bring you back to a more positive frequency and then you are free to start moving up the high-vibrational ladder again. Every time you move your focus to that high-vibrational, 'having' place, you are doing something proactive towards changing your life and achieving your dreams. We can all feel energy changes in our bodies as we go about our day and I highly recommend that you tune into your inner world and start asking yourself questions around these:

- What triggered me?

- What changed it?

- What just happened?

- When did it change?

- What was I doing at that time?

- What was I thinking or feeling?
- Has this come from me or someone else's energy field?

Remember, there is no blame here (and we are all connected anyway), but sometimes we just pick up free-floating thoughts and imprinted feelings. Release them and let them go if they don't belong to you.

Taking time out to reflect on my business and journaling, meditating, practising breathwork and EFT whenever I feel a build-up of negative emotions in my head is a fundamental part of my life now. To me, flow means understanding that I can't *push* myself to work twelve-hour days anymore and my business model reflects that. Understanding that I need to take enjoyable breaks that bring me real pleasure (and kick the guilt) and keeping an open dialogue between my mind and body through daily meditation helps me to stay in flow. Flow is energy, and that's what I am acutely tuned into now. It tells me everything I need to know. If your life is not working, then look to your energy for the answers.

Burnout and the mind

When we get to a burnt-out or exhausted state, our energy field is depleted and it needs replenishing before we can do anything else. Most of us are already working from a state of empty or near-empty. We work hard on increasing our energy or mojo by just a bit, and when we feel better we start overworking again and go back to empty. Changing the way you think can help. Instead of using your mind to think, plan or do, try going through the heart. Allow your heart to guide you. The heart replenishes our energy by creating and increasing the electromagnetic field around our physical body. Let the heart's energy field heal you and bring you back to happy.

This will probably feel hard to do at the beginning, because we are not used to using our heart in the modern world, but once you get the hang of it, it will change your life, energy and health because it will start to magnetise your energy field again. When working with people I have noticed that not only are many of them blocked in their hearts, but there is little understanding of how it can help them have better lives or businesses. Leading from the heart is the same thing as trusting or 'surrendering' to the universe, because the heart, higher mind and universe (energy field) are all interconnected. It's about letting the ego go and transcending the mind (often called the death of the ego) and forms part of The Hero's Journey, which I suspect we are all on.[137] Allow yourself to be guided by your joy, pleasure, passion and excitement. Don't over-plan. If you are not used to feeling happy and enjoying your life or you are exhausted then this will feel alien to you, but give yourself permission to live life in this way. Not only is the heart full of wisdom, but it's also your guiding light. Remember that your brain is being guided by the heart anyway – you are simply bringing your awareness back to this way of living and being so you can hear or feel the heart too. Try this exercise below to incorporate heart-focused meditation into your life.

EXERCISE: Heart-Focused Meditation

Breathe deeply and close your eyes. Pull your attention back behind the eyes and allow any free-floating thoughts, worries or anxieties to float past. Now bring your awareness to your heart. Feel into your heart and feel those warm feelings begin to flow. Feel the love and compassion for yourself and others in your heart and start to push this love out of yourself. Then push it out into the room. Now push it out of the house. Then the city. Then the planet. Then the universe. Feel it spreading across the entire cosmos, lighting up everything as it flows.

Now pull your awareness back into your heart again. What feels right or good for your heart? Ask your heart questions and feel into it. If your mind keeps getting in the way then you can turn down the dial as you did in the higher mind meditation. The heart is connected to the higher mind because they are both connected to the energy field via your high-vibrational energy.

Don't force your goals

I often get approached by people who ask me why they haven't achieved their dreams or goals yet, even though they are working so hard. My answer is always this: don't force your goals or dreams, because this is the wrong energy. Keep the connection to your higher self and heart as open as possible using techniques such as meditating, journaling, divination tools and writing down your dreams while being aware of divine timing. Always keep your big vision in your mind so that you know where you are going and why (for motivation). Try and enjoy your business and life while focusing on your next step. Your higher self, inner wisdom or the heart can tell you what it wants (your vision or goals), but it can't give you the exact steps on how to get there because each step is dependent on the last. It's a bit like doing a jigsaw puzzle. You must follow the steps to get to the end, but there are multiple ways and variations on how to get there. That's the joy of life: we get to choose what we want.

If you dread getting out of bed each morning knowing that you have to go to a business or job you hate, then you are not living in alignment with your heart or your higher self and these feelings will only get worse. You don't have to walk away from your business or job, but getting back to basics regarding your vision and becoming energetically realigned is fundamental. Your energy is out of sync, and that could just as easily be your business as you. Remember, everything has an energetic blueprint – your business, you, your workspace, your house, your spouse and your kids.

Energetic alignment

When the heart and mind are coherent, the body is in energetic alignment, but how can we use this technique to get our life and business into alignment? Energetic alignment is when you are vibrating at the frequency of everything that your soul and heart desires and you are spiritually, mentally, physically, emotionally and environmentally aligned. Essentially, you have worked (or are working) through the limiting beliefs, thought patterns and limitations holding you back and you are now connected to your soul and can hear what it wants to do. Every time you get triggered, it is an opportunity to figure out what triggered you so that you can release the energy and raise your vibration again. Not only does this help you to reframe daily frustrations and stressors, but it also helps you to get back to your soul's purpose (or what you want to do in this life, if soul's purpose doesn't resonate with you). The more we release trapped, low-vibrational energy, the closer we get to true fulfilment and meaning. Once you combine purpose, genius, meaning, passion, vision and mission with determination and grit, you have a winning formula for continued business success and true happiness in your life. It can be hard to maintain, but you just have to keep realigning yourself when you go off-kilter (which will happen, as you are living in a physical body in a 3D world).

Energetic alignment is essentially about the five pillars of vibration we outlined in the last chapter. Each pillar needs to have an aligned energetic harmony of its own and there must be energetic harmony between them all: mind, body, soul, heart and energy. They all work together. By working through our childhood traumas, ancestral abuse and judgements of life, we release limited thinking and trapped energy skewing our vibrational frequency, and blocking our energy channels and centres, until we eventually get down to the core of our souls' purpose or mission or our hearts' desires. Alternatively, we can use reiki, energy healing, crystal alchemy or other energy techniques to get ourselves vibrationally aligned and return the flow of energy in the right direction through our energy centres or chakras. This lets consciousness flow through, bringing new wisdom and creative inspiration so we can find increased clarity and hear our souls whisper again. Energy or consciousness will always take the path of least resistance through the body, so the fewer blockages there are, the more your whole body will benefit from the upgrades of the higher consciousness of the energy field.

There is one last aspect of energetic alignment, and that's action. Energy always needs a direction and needs to move, so the last piece of the energetic puzzle is to take aligned action on your desires, which brings them into reality. In a sense, it's the action which brings your energy into alignment or sets the frequency off so it can be realised in the energy field. Try this exercise to help get yourself energetically aligned.

EXERCISE: Energetically Aligning Yourself

Take five deep breaths and close your eyes. Relax and release the chatter of the physical world. Imagine you are sitting on a secluded beach with white sands and blue sea. You can smell the salty water, feel the warm sand and hear the waves crashing on the shore. Let all the thoughts go from your mind. Bring your attention to your breath and feel yourself breathing in and out. Now bring your attention to your heart and feel the warm glow starting to build up around it. Sit in silence and feel into your body, heart and mind. Allow yourself to feel at one with the universe and have gratitude for your life so you can access the higher brainwave states. Begin to pull energy up from the ground, through your feet, up through your body, the seven chakras and then up into the 8th chakra – the higher mind. Notice the higher mind as a swirling white ball of light. When you feel relaxed and expanded inside, then you can start asking questions about your life and business.

Here are some example questions from my own business, but let your energy and higher mind guide you on which questions to ask:

- What do I need in my life right now?

- What will make my soul feel proud?

- What is the right direction for my heart?

- How would my heart solve this problem?

- What is the message my higher mind is trying to send me today?

- What is stopping me from hearing what my soul wants?

- What am I open to receiving today?

- Is my business aligned with my soul?

- Do I feel worthy of living my soul's purpose?

- How can I align my services with my heart?

- How can I find clarity today?

- What is the next step in my business?

- How do I achieve mind, body and soul alignment in my business or life?

- What do I need to let go from my life or business to create more room for opportunity?

- Am I allowing myself to receive more abundance and prosperity in my life?

- Am I sabotaging my own success? How?

Stepping into your own power

I discovered that when I started setting boundaries in my business, it raised my own frequency, which in turn made a positive impact on my life. Stepping into your power is so much more than just setting boundaries, though. It's also about:

- Planning and managing yourself and others.

- Taking charge, taking responsibility and taking inspired action.

- Not people pleasing.

- Working through your to-do list (and making it manageable in the first place).

- Outsourcing what you don't want to do.

- Taking care of yourself, taking time off and putting yourself first.

- Believing in yourself and your dreams and taking pride in what you do.

- Refusing to work with difficult people and walking away from people that leave you feeling bad about yourself or drained.

It's anything that allows you to prioritise your energy and yourself in your own life. Stepping up and taking charge of your life is probably the single most important thing you can do, because it shifts your energy so fast. The problem is that not prioritising yourself is still a form of self-sabotage or unworthiness: you need to put your own oxygen mask on before you put it on anyone else. Not loving yourself fully and completely will stop you behaving in a way that prioritises your own power and belief in yourself.

I walked into my marriage as a strong, career-orientated, intelligent woman and then promptly gave my power away to my husband (who didn't even know what to do with it). It took me years to realise that I was simply following the pre-programming downloaded from my parents (and even ancestors), but by then I had already created the wrong dynamic in my marriage. I have had time to repair and rewire it, but when dealing with customers, potential love matches, line managers and more, you don't have ten years to get things right, so my advice is always to set boundaries from the start. To set boundaries properly, you have to be aware of your energy and how you are playing out the stories of your ancestors. You also have to be aware of others' energies, which you can feel if you are aware enough. You can feel those undermining remarks hidden behind a smile on a first date. You can feel if your line manager feels threatened by your passion and enthusiasm (although you may not be able to prove it) and you can feel when a potential customer is being unreasonable. You can also feel when you have just given your power away to someone else, because you feel weak, small, powerless or insignificant.

You don't have to feel any of those things, because you can claim your power back. We claim our power back with our choices and reactions to situations, and the more we do it, the better we get at it. A small portion of the reality of our lives comes from experiences and situations, the remainder comes from our reactions to these situations. Walk away from that first date with your head held high, find a win/win solution with that customer or not at all, and be more empathetic to your line manager with your choice of words, because the reality of our lives always starts with us. You can always leave that job and the 'projecting' line manager, but in the meantime, your awareness and grasp of the true reason for their behaviour gives you immense power over the situation and helps you to be more compassionate and patient until you are ready to leave.

It's also important to release any resentment, grudges, bitterness, regrets or even thoughts of revenge from your mind, because these are all low-vibrational energies which are pulling you down. There are many techniques you can use, such as writing a letter to the person telling them how they made you feel (and then burning it), practising daily forgiveness mantras for at least a month to start rewiring your subconscious mind or visualising you and this person talking it through and apologising to each other and maybe even hugging if it's someone close. Remember, visualisation is just as real for your mind as if it has really happened, allowing your subconscious to get closure so you can move on. Depending on how deep-rooted it is, you may need to repeat these techniques, just allow yourself to be guided by your heart and soul.

EIGHT

The Power Of Us

Our conscious reality tells us that we are individual beings because this is how our ego sees the world, but through the lens of energy, we are completely connected. From an energetic viewpoint, we are clusters of energy that look like clusters of light and we are all joined together by energy waves. Even the space between your desk and chair isn't really empty space – it's energy waves ebbing and flowing around you. Try standing up and moving your hands in a scissor shape around you. I bet it makes you feel more energised and raring to go. That's because you have shaken the energy around you, so any energetic stagnation you may have had is now gone (but it will come back if you don't change your thoughts, beliefs and words).

Everything in our ever-expanding universe is made up of, or emits, light and information or energy and consciousness. Everything is energy and information. Our bodies are made up of gravitationally-organised light filled with frequencies. They continuously send and receive these frequencies.[138]

The collective consciousness

Carl Jung first referred to the collective unconscious in 1916, so it's not a new concept,[139] but with the discovery of mirror neurons, maybe we can get a practical view of what this is as we see glimpses of the energy field entangling to enhance humans as a social species – one that needs to learn to coexist and work together. Mirror-neuron systems are thought to play a part in empathy – imitating the actions of others, understanding intentions and feeling another's pain. However, research is starting to show that they are less 'nature' and more 'nurture' and are not necessarily genetically inherited, but we develop them, possibly when there is a 'cultural' need.[140] Could this be zeitgeists of change from the quantum field?

I believe that we are all picking up each other's feelings, thoughts and emotions all the time and often taking them on as our own. If we aren't even aware that we can do this, we certainly won't know which of these aren't ours. Possessing this knowledge can really help you to live a better life, because once you know that these aren't your emotions, but someone else's, you can clear your energy field and get back to being 'you' again. This is an area known as emotional contagion, where we pick up or become the emotions of others. Growing studies on the behaviour of kindness, such as 'pay it forward' schemes, are showing that kindness is infectious. When we act kinder to others around us, these people are not only more likely to act kinder to us, but also behave in a kinder way to those they meet afterwards.[141] This is particularly common amongst children, especially if their parents are kind. We can change the world around us, with our own actions and feelings.

Our brain doesn't hold much data

In Steven Sloman and Philip Fernbach's book *The Knowledge Illusion: The myth of individual thought and the power of collective wisdom*, they state that our brains do not have the ability to remember much information. We only have approximately 1GB of storage space in our memories and minds, but when we work together, we create amazing things because we spark off each other. We don't have to remember everything, because those around us will fill in the gaps and when we create teams, communities and networks, we excel.[142] My belief is that it's not just other people's neurons we are sparking off – our own electromagnetic energy fields are entangling and sharing information and downloading creativity and ideas from the living, breathing quantum field as well. When we learn more from reading, taking courses, researching, etc, we also spark our brains into remembering more, because doing this actually changes our biology. Neurons are designed to connect and the mind looks for patterns everywhere, so whether connecting with others, connecting with ourselves or connecting with the energy field, it's all going to help you live a better life and build a more successful business in the process.

Working with others doubles the speed

Because we are all energetically connected, we can jump on the bandwagon of someone else's deep inner work too. If your own energy work is taking a while or it feels like slow progress, then try working with others. This is probably one of the biggest benefits of us being energetically connected: when you change, it affects the others around you too and when they change, evolve and grow, it will also affect you. This is why group training can work so well, especially if it's a training session where we are intrinsically developing ourselves in some way. We start to energetically connect with each other's energy fields and work on those underlying beliefs, ancestral beliefs or societal conditioning at the same time. Essentially, the group evolves together.

The same can be said for listening to someone's podcast, reading their posts and books or watching their videos. You are not just entangling with the words they speak; you are entangling with everything in their energy field too, so the more learning and research you do, the more you are initiated and activated into their way of thinking and being (which may or may not be beneficial, depending on who you follow).

Building communities

Around the world there are certain 'blue zones' which boast the largest numbers of centenarians amongst the world's population, with Okinawa, Japan famously having the most. Having researched these little pockets around the world – ranging from Sardinia, to Greece, and even California – researchers have found certain similarities. Obviously, diet and lifestyle play a huge part, as does having a purpose, but interestingly, so does community. Three of these five areas are islands so community has always been an important part of their lives, but after studying the inhabitants of Okinawa, researchers saw first-hand how vital community was for the wellbeing of its inhabitants. They now feel it is one of the key reasons why this island boasts the highest amount of people over the age of 100.

On the island, the inhabitants are all assigned a group to be a part of from birth. Not only do they grow up together, but they are all assigned individual tasks that they carry out for the duration of their lives together. The research showed that fun, laughter, singing and dancing formed an important part of their lives, as did meeting up with friends, neighbours and their groups every day to perform activities or drink tea together and chat. The islanders all report that having these close relationships and being part of this community helps to give them more meaning and purpose in their lives. It's not just about them, it's also about helping others in their group, which can often be a powerful motivator.[143]

Communities help us to live longer and to be healthier and happier and yet the current world we live in is moving us away from them. It is clear to me that we need to move back to communities if we are to thrive. In my opinion, face-to-face is always better, but I'm not too sure that our world is moving in that direction anymore. Social media is a tool that we can use to build communities, but it can be difficult and take longer, so we need to find our own way of doing it. Ultimately, it has to work with your energy for it to work for you. For example, if you are someone that doesn't like selling, feels resistance when you are about to pick up the phone, or hates connecting with people on social media, then reframing all of these as relationship-building actions can be a good way of viewing them. The joy of connecting with others is hard to beat, so reframing your mind around what these mean to you can be hugely helpful and even make it enjoyable.

The reality is that people can feel when you are selling to them and don't like it and social media has made us all a lot more suspicious. As a society we are increasingly waking up to our energetic side and underhand methods are switching people off as we get wise to their tricks. Think about the types of people you are happy to buy from and ask yourself why. They are likely the more genuine, transparent and authentic ones.

It always surprises people to learn that true networking is not about us at all. It's about what we can do for others. Studies already show us that people are more likely to buy from us if they like us, or when we help them out first. If they don't, it's probably because they are exhausted, desperate or have limiting beliefs around it (or they can sense or don't trust your real motives) and can't see the wood for the trees anymore. They have lost that wonderful human part of themselves, but you can remind them of it by treating them in a positive and caring way.

Douglas Rushkoff, producer and host of the Team Human podcast believes that we are programmed to collaborate and work together.[144] We are a social species and when we are not able to connect with others, we start to feel uninspired, demotivated and negative. Judgements, criticism, envy and the competitive self comes out and our mind starts to see the world in a negative way. Certainly, when I first moved overseas with young children and dived massively into social media as a way to meet other mums and cope with being a new mum, I had no clue how much it would affect my mental state. Back then, I had no idea I was attracting people, situations and experiences (albeit online) based on my subconscious programming and thinking.

In retrospect, it has worked out well because I have now created awareness and eliminated decades of self-sabotaging, but as I look at the amount of support groups that have opened up around mental health and being a stay-at-home mum, I can see I am not the only one that struggled with this. With this in mind, start connecting and building relationships and leave the expectations behind. Try to see the relationship or connection itself as the end goal. This new connection may become a business partner, a lifelong friend or a new customer. You don't need to know what the end result is going to be. This is the essence of living an energetic life: releasing the expectation, the control and the fixed way of doing things and letting life flow a bit more.

Trusting in your higher self is vital. Always remember that your higher self knows what your heart wants (even if you don't) and is doing its best to take you there. As long as you know what your soul wants and can occasionally pick up on its whispers through meditation, signs or 'aha' moments, then trust that this is the direction that your higher self is leading you in. The laws of physics are the laws of nature. Since we can't control nature, we are far better off letting things flow a bit more naturally and instead focus on sitting in elevated frequencies more often. There is no pressure, there is no struggle, there is no desperation; it's only your current state of being that is creating any of that. Change your state of being and change your life.

Entangling with others in the energy field

The collective consciousness is not just downloading or channelling energy from the energy field around us; it's also entangling with the energy fields of others, which is something we are always doing. Say, for example, you are sitting in a meeting. You want to say something, but you are too worried about what other people will think. Suddenly, someone says exactly what you were going to say. The second you think it (or 'download' it), it's in your energy field. Now it's going to be open for other people to become aware of it, albeit subconsciously. Trust in yourself and say it before someone else does. This is the connection between us, inside the energy field, and also how we are regularly 'downloading' ideas and inspiration all the time.

There are many cases of people coming up with the same ideas, book covers, business names, inventions and music at the same time. Complete strangers on opposite sides of the world have tried to patent the same invention on the same day. We access each other's energy fields through awareness, so it is our subconscious mind that picks up the ideas and thoughts of others. We often don't even know that we are doing it. We don't pick up these messages and signals with our five senses, or even our conscious mind; we pick them up with our subconscious mind. We think they come from us, but we are all 'reading' each other's minds or energy fields continuously. It's a normal part of who we are – we just aren't aware of it.

Collective positive energy

Positive energy is a vibration, and something we desperately need more of in this world. We can raise the energies of our world (and universe) by collectively raising our own energies. There are many groups already doing this in the world, such as Unify,[145] Nassim Haramein's Resonance Science Foundation[146] and Joe Dispenza's Project Coherence,[147] to name a few. More importantly, we know for a fact that raising a community's collective positive vibration actually works. The World Peace Group are one of many groups of meditators who use transcendental meditation to reduce crime. Two such studies involve Washington, US in 1993 and Liverpool, UK between 1978 and 1991, where controlled studies were carried out to reduce the crime rate. Results were varied, but both showed that crime was reduced. In Washington, petty crime dropped by 23.3%.[148] In Liverpool, the crime rate dropped by 58% over five years (but it took ten years to show significant changes and it required an increase to 1% of the population meditating).[149] Their results were not perfect, but it's a start.

The human mind is able to achieve powerful results during meditation and one thing is certain: the more people that join, the better the results and the more we will all thrive. It is my belief that we can also do this with money and increase the collective wealth of entire nations. For example, recently I went to transfer money between countries but discovered that the market had massively dropped. I was annoyed with myself for not keeping an eye on the exchange rates, but it got me thinking that if we can change our DNA, reduce crime rates and eliminate disease with the power of our minds, then maybe we can improve the financial markets, too. I suspect that there are probably people already doing this, whoever is directing consciousness in a stronger way at that time (high-vibrational energy is stronger than lower-vibrational energy) will direct the flow of money, but as it involves many different variables around the world, we would need to do this as a larger group.

Currently, Unify are working on creating a 'tipping' effect in the world, which is known as the Maharishi effect.[150] The aim is to get 1% of the world's population to raise their frequency or level of consciousness through meditation and then the rest of the world will 'tip' upwards energetically. According to Dr David Hawkins in *Truth Vs. Falsehood: How to Tell the Difference,* we have already achieved this. Using his levels of consciousness model, which is based on 20 years of research, Hawkins states that in 2003 humanity raised its collective consciousness up to 207 and into the level of collective courage. But it was only 15% of humanity that did this; 85% of humanity are still below the level of courage (207) and thus at the levels of pride, anger, desire (through the ego, not the heart), fear, grief, apathy, guilt, shame etc.[151] If 15% of the world can affect the other 85% then this gives me great hope, enabling more of us to start living happier and more fulfilling lives; something which my heart truly wants to see before I leave this planet. I want to know that all the children in the world are living in a better, and happier, world. We can create this better world with our own vibrational frequency.

For a variety of reasons, the world has been too negative for too long – negative news sells, scary films get our hormones flowing and are addictive and we are all living more stressful lives, signalling the 'fight or flight' hormones. Our minds are more disposed to focus on negative thoughts, and fear and worry is passed down in our DNA. With two world wars, genocide, extreme poverty, persecution and ancestral abuse included in our family lines, a lot of trauma and fear has been passed down with it. Humanity's leanings towards negativity are creating a negative environment for all of us. Suicide rates are on the rise and our children are becoming depressed, sad and negative. If you truly want to make a bigger impact on the world around you, then this is one of the easiest ways to do it. Raise your own level of consciousness – feel the love inside your heart and radiate it outwards into the world around you – and impact all the people around you so that they can raise theirs.

Our brains create the reality that we live in, yet we are all connected through consciousness. By working together to create a more positive and less fearful world we can increase the vibrations of the world, and universe, around us. Connect with your inner and energetic self again, feel positive, radiate outwards with a loving heart, and work on your own limitations. Change the world for the good of our children. It really is this simple, and the more of us that do this, the faster the world will change.

Together, we are stronger.

Conclusion

This book has been a story of following my heart (knowing) over my mind (ego) – something that took me a long time to learn. I had worked in business for so long, and I am an extremely practical person. I had literally shut down the spiritual or energetic aspects of myself (and my heart) and got caught up in the overthinking, worrying, over-critical aspects of being human. I was so energetically contracted with fear, worry and social conditioning that I was living a half-life. Remembering that I am a multidimensional person with multiple facets, talents and abilities has helped me to step back into an energetically expanded and more enjoyable life again.

I remember lying on my back in the park staring up at the night sky. I'd see flashing lights circling around and think, 'I didn't know that stars moved like that,' or see balls of light flashing past above my head and wonder what they were. I spent my childhood dreaming of flying around the house and I've taken on a whole lifetime of other people's thoughts and emotions as my own, because it never even occurred to me that they weren't mine. These experiences don't seem so strange anymore, because I have raised my levels of consciousness to a new way of being and am channelling in more beneficial energy or consciousness for me.

My mind is now completely open and expanded. In my meditations I have been able to connect with higher consciousness energies or frequencies (or deeper parts of me), including some which really resonated with my heart, but I had to become attuned to this first. It didn't happen overnight. It has to be a slow process because our brains need to work on peeling back our belief structures first and many of us are in denial of things we can't see. I am not saying this is wrong, but I recommend learning to feel or sense things instead, because there is so much 'around us' that we can't see; plus it will teach us to trust ourselves more, which will help us thrive in this 3D world. What I know in my heart to be true is that we live in a multidimensional universe/s with trillions of other civilisations that we can connect to as soon as we wake up to the possibility of it. We are surrounded by pure consciousness, pure love, and even other family members from the past, present and future who I suspect are trying to connect with us too.

Writing this book has been some journey. I had to develop so much trust in myself and my intuition, which is why I lost my way so many times. My mind wanted to write what it knows (and with thirty years of business under its belt, it knows a lot), but my heart knew that it needed to write something different. As you can see, I followed my heart, soul and intuition and this is the way I live my life too. Heart or intuition first, mind later. In my opinion, life and business have to come from the inside out, otherwise we just don't feel fulfilled and could even end up taking the wrong path – one that we feel we *should* be taking, rather than the one we *want* to take.

Having a masters in a people development subject I know that goals have to be intrinsic or come from the heart, but what I couldn't see was that fear was keeping me stuck inside the collective consciousness of others. It was preventing me from connecting to my soul and seeing what I really wanted to do in life, let alone allowing me to start creating heartfelt strategies to get there. For me, setting ego-based goals in life and then creating strategies to work towards them just felt meaningless and not only compounded my own depression, but made my life feel pointless and disappointing. Once I started hearing my inner voice or higher self, I could find true purpose and meaning in life, but it had to unfold in its own way, which is why patience is required. When we align ourselves to our true path (values and purpose) in life, and then adopt the frequency of courage to commit to walking this path, things can escalate quickly and we can be amazed at how fast our lives can change.

When we start to see phenomena like balls of light or orbs, we are seeing more of the energetic world around us, and this is a sign that we are becoming more enlightened or 'waking up'. It's always been there; we just couldn't see it because we can only see a small portion of what's around us and our brains also filter out what they don't believe. Dreaming of flying around the house is simply our consciousness exploring (and seeing) more of the energy field while we sleep. This is remote viewing and we can do it while we are awake too. Studies carried out with children and adults across the world are demonstrating that we don't need our eyes to see, or even read, as we can do this with our mind's eye.[152] We may need to learn how to do it but we can *all* do it. As you can imagine, this provides a lot of hope to those who are visually impaired.

As mad as all this may sound, I gratefully carry on walking this path that began with my grief, pain, depression, the near-end of my marriage, burnout, and trying to be a better mum for my children but failing miserably. Luckily, thanks to neuroplasticity, I am also managing to rewire my family's minds back to happy by adopting more 'conscious parenting' practices and observing their actions and words to see where they may have picked up their own (or my) limiting beliefs.

From my ongoing meditating and channelling sessions, I now understand that the message of our day is to be free, empowered and connecting with higher consciousness so that we can live our dreams. Consciousness flows through us physically and energetically and loves us beyond anything that our imaginations can ever comprehend, because we truly don't understand what the word love means. It means expansion, connection, courage, compassion and truth.

I have learned that humans are not supposed to be perfect, but they are supposed to be living a better life than the one that most of us are living. Emotions are essentially the energy that drives us. Life without emotions would be grey indeed, but learning to manage our emotions and trust ourselves and inner wisdom is a good place to start. Don't pressure yourself. Take it slow and focus on living a more enjoyable life and pushing this joy and love out into the world around you, because just doing that is enough. The more you push love out of your body, the more you push negative or low-vibrational energy out of your body, which in turn fills the world up with your higher-vibrational state.

If you have wounds, limiting beliefs or low-vibrational frequencies trapped in your energy field, then you can work to unpick those using the tools in this book, alongside doing reiki, energy healing, bioenergetic frequency healing and as many DNA activations and attunements as you can to energetically release stagnation from your field while becoming more conscious of your own limited stories and patterns. If you are a perfectionist, worrier and workaholic like I used to be, then maybe this will help:

> You are exactly where you are supposed to be in your life and everything is working out in the way it is meant to. Most of your experiences have led you to this point and are relevant to where you want to go next, because your higher mind has been guiding you even if you aren't aware of it. Follow your heart. Trust in yourself. Notice the subtle signs and messages from the energy field around you. Practise meditation and journaling when you can to eliminate all that conditioning and get back to the 'real you'. Connect with others, but don't dilute yourself in the process. Above all, be kind to yourself and know that you are never alone. Ask for help around you. We are all connected and you only have to be your authentic self to start attracting more people like you.

Love, Ruth Elisabeth

Afterword

Since the late 1980s, the earth has been slowly raising her own vibration as she starts to move into what has often been referred to as the 5th dimension. It's not a place to go; it's a state of being. Essentially, the range of frequencies that make up our unique frequency (or the frequency of the planet) have all raised up to a higher bandwidth. We are currently in the 3rd or 4th (or even 5th for some enlightened people) dimension/density, depending on where your levels of consciousness are, but the earth has been moving towards the 5th for quite some time. On 21 December 2019, our planet moved into a new position in the solar system, which has helped to raise her own vibration yet again. This increase in vibrational resonance has caused new, higher-vibrational cosmic energy to bombard our planet, raising the collective vibration of the earth. Because we are part of this planet and the global energy network, we are energetically tuned into, and resonate with, the planet's atmosphere. Our collective consciousness resonates among us, but also with planet earth. With the new research around collective networks of consciousness, it's looking like we have all collectively created this planet together (or the planet has energetically created us) – whether consciously aware of this or not.[153]

These new higher energies are said to act as an activation, attunement or initiation for our bodies by switching on dormant DNA. These frequencies or energies are beginning to activate our bodies, bringing them up into a higher-vibrational state, which will allow lower-vibrational energies to start naturally falling away. We already know the healing effects of sound (frequency), so maybe this is why so many of us are beginning to feel different now? We are literally starting to wake up and see, sense and feel more of what's around us. The environment – and the new energies – are changing us from the inside out as we evolve into a 'higher-vibrational' and more 'expanded' species. We need to help Mother Nature out though, by working on ourselves and our negative or low-vibrational, trapped emotions and beliefs, as these emotions are affecting the collective consciousness of humans and our planet.

As soon as we raise our own frequency, we will be more energy and light and our lives will start to work better for us. We will experience more harmony and be more connected to our true, multidimensional selves. I suspect that depression will disappear for many of us too. Life will flow better and feel easier, because many of the low-vibrational forces, resistance or energies will not be able to exist in this higher dimension anymore (we are now out of their frequency range). Of course, there will still be disagreements, annoyances and emotional outbursts because we are humans, not robots, but we will be living more intentionally, more consciously and more compassionately than we have been before, which will help our world thrive.

We are moving into a new paradigm as our understanding and acceptance of consciousness as the energy field shifts us into a new way of viewing humanity and our place in this world. The physical world that we live in has been created by us within the collective consciousness, so we have the power to shift it into anything that we want to experience. We can create global negative experiences or we can create global positive experiences – the power lies within us – and we all have more power than we know.

We have been given the gift of free will and free thought so that we can co-create something that even transcends consciousness. We can dance with consciousness and be inspired to take our bodies and minds to new realms. We can sing with consciousness and be inspired to create new music that heals our bodies, releases energy and connects us with other dimensions. We can learn or dream with consciousness and then relish in new philosophies and ancient memories that stream into our minds. As long as we don't connect to low-vibrational thoughts, energies and frequencies, I truly believe it is helping our lives two-fold. Others who have passed before us still want to help us, and this is what I believe 'higher consciousness' entities are. Yes, our physical bodies eventually die in this low-density, 3D reality (although we can certainly live longer than we are doing now), but we still live on as an energy source and maintain our essence and truth.

The current message of the universe is to let these low-vibrational thoughts, energies and frequencies go from our lives and to know that we are supported by many higher consciousness entities (frequencies), because they come from other planets, dimensions and realms too. We are surrounded by others who want to help us (and have been doing so for millennia), we simply need to turn our attention to them. Our world has been low-vibrational and fearful for too long, but this is changing as the cosmos floods the planet with higher-vibrational energies and frequencies to lift all of us up into our innate and abundant state. For many of us, this will take some faith (and probably some inner work), but it's not faith in something outside of us – it's faith in us, because unconditional love is who we are.

The universe that we live in is incredible and now that I am completely aware of this, life feels better. Not only do I feel supported and guided, but my heart has stopped feeling anxious because I know who I am, where I'm going and why. I have a vision and a mission that helps to give more meaning and purpose to my life, but I have true flexibility within this to create whatever I feel called to create that day and not be bound by expectation anymore. I feel that there is a sort of order to this universe (I cannot say how or why), although I appreciate that I may never get the absolute answers to these sorts of questions until my physical body dies and I become consciousness again and open to all the knowledge that there is in the universe. I do know that to even experience these sorts of emotional dialogues with your higher mind, and beyond, you have to be completely in your own sovereignty, trust yourself and your heart completely and be out of your own fear or judgement. These experiences have enriched my life, body and mind in ways that I could never have foreseen (and I didn't even have to leave my house).

Life is never about being perfect; it's about having the tools to get you through the hard parts. Trust in your innate abilities, intuitive gifts and supernatural talents because you are filled to the brim with them. We *all* are, and they are beginning to bubble up to the surface for all of us now as the world starts to shift and evolve.

References

1. Dispenza, J, *Becoming Supernatural: How common people are doing the uncommon* (Hay House, 2017), p 92
2. Einstein Exhibition, 'Quantum theory', American Museum of Natural History (no date), www.amnh.org/exhibitions/einstein/legacy/quantum-theory, accessed 10 December 2021
3. Webb, R, 'Quantum Physics: Our best basic picture of how particles interact to make the world', *New Scientist* (no date), www.newscientist.com/term/quantum-physics, accessed 10 December 2021
4. Kaku, M, *Hyperspace: A scientific odyssey through parallel universes, time warps, and the tenth dimension* (OUP Oxford, 2016), pp 111–112
5. Letzter, R, 'Giant Molecules Exist in Two Places at Once in Unprecedented Quantum Experiment', *Scientific American* (October 2019), www.scientificamerican.com/article/giant-molecules-exist-in-two-places-at-once-in-unprecedented-quantum-experiment, accessed 28 December 2021
6. Weizmann Institute of Science, 'Quantum Theory Demonstrated: Observation Affects Reality', *ScienceDaily* (27 February 1998), www.sciencedaily.com/releases/1998/02/980227055013.htm, accessed 10 December 2021
7. Siegel, E, 'Ask Ethan: Are Quantum Fields Real?', *Forbes* (17 November 2018), www.forbes.com/sites/startswithabang/2018/11/17/ask-ethan-are-quantum-fields-real/?sh=2e79ddf8777a, accessed 10 December 2021

8. Mullen, L, 'Plasma, plasma, everywhere' (*Nasa Science*, 7 September 1999), https://science.nasa.gov/science-news/science-at-nasa/1999/ast07sep99_1, accessed 10 December 2021

9. McTaggart, L, *The Field: The quest for the secret force of the universe* (HarperCollins, 2001), Ch 5, pp 97–126

10. Seth, A, 'Your brain hallucinates your conscious reality', TedTalk (2017), www.youtube.com/watch?v=lyu7v7nWzfo&t=364s, accessed 2 January 2022

11. Farnsworth, B, 'How to Measure Emotions and Feelings (And the Difference Between Them)', IMOTIONS (14 April 2020), https://imotions.com/blog/difference-feelings-emotions, accessed 10 December 2021

12. Garland, E, et al, 'Upward Spirals of Positive Emotions Counter Downward Spirals of Negativity: Insights from the broaden-and-build theory and affective neuroscience on the treatment of emotion dysfunctions and deficits in psychopathology' (*Clinical Psychology Review*, November 2010), www.ncbi.nlm.nih.gov/pmc/articles/PMC2908186, accessed 10 December 2021

13. Emoto, M, *The Hidden Messages in Water* (Atrio Books, 2004)

14. Stokes, H and Ward, K, 'Emotions Are Energy: The bodymind connection and e-motion', Authenticity Associates blog (28 August 2012), www.authenticityassociates.com/emotions-are-energy, accessed 28 December 2021

15. Pegg, M, 'Jill Bolte Taylor: My Stroke of Insight', The Positive Encourager blog, www.thepositiveencourager.global/jill-bolte-taylors-stroke-of-insight-video-2, accessed 28 December 2021

16. Lipton, B, *The Honeymoon Effect: The science of creating heaven on earth* (Hay House, 2015); *Spontaneous Evolution: Our positive future (and a way to get there from here)* (Hay House, 2011); *The Biology of Belief: Unleashing the power of consciousness, matter & miracles* (Hay House, 2011)

17. Cosmos, 'Constructive interference', https://astronomy.swin.edu.au/cosmos/c/Constructive+Interference, accessed 28 December 2021

18. Lipton, B, 'Inner Evolution: Quantum Perceptions of Matter', Series 1, Episode 3 (Gaia, March 2020), www.gaia.com/video/quantum-perceptions-matter, accessed 26 December 2021

19. Crowther, J, *Oxford Advanced Learner's Dictionary of Current English*, 5th Edition (Oxford University Press, 1995), p 244

20. Rubik, B, et al, 'Science and Healing: History, Terminology, and Concepts' (*Global Advances in Health and Medicine*, November 2015), www.ncbi.nlm.nih.gov/pmc/articles/PMC4654789, accessed 10 December 2021

21. Fraser, J, 'How the Human Body Creates Electromagnetic Fields', *Forbes* (November 2017), www.forbes.com/sites/quora/2017/11

/03/how-the-human-body-creates-electromagnetic-fields/?sh=
53580ddb56ea, accessed 10 December 2021

22. Lipton, B, 'Inner Evolution: Quantum Perceptions of Matter',
Series 1, Episode 3 (Gaia, March 2020), www.gaia.com/video
/quantum-perceptions-matter, accessed 26 December 2021

23. HeartMath Institute, 'Exploring the Role of the Heart in Human
Performance: Energetic Communication' (HeartMath Institute,
no date), Chapter 6, www.heartmath.org/research/science-of-the
-heart/energetic-communication, accessed 10 December 2021

24. The HeartMath Experience, 'The Science of The Heart', Series
1, Episode 3 (Gaia, 2020), www.gaia.com/video/science-heart,
accessed 10 December 2021

25. Arianrhod, R, 'Einstein, Bohr and the origins of entanglement',
Cosmos Weekly (October 2017), https://cosmosmagazine.com
/science/physics/einstein-bohr-and-the-origins-of-entanglement,
accessed 10 December 2021

26. CERN Institute: https://home.cern

27. Pomeroy, R, 'The Most Astounding Fact in the Universe',
RealClear Science (4 March 2012), www.realclearscience.com/blog
/2012/03/the-most-astounding-fact-in-the-universe.html, accessed
10 December 2021

28. McFadden, J, 'Integrating Information In The Brain's Em
Field: The cemi field theory of consciousness' (*Neuroscience of
Consciousness*, October 2020), https://doi.org/10.1093/nc/niaa016

29. Radboud University Nijmegen, 'Brain works like a radio receiver',
ScienceDaily (22 January 2014), www.sciencedaily.com/releases
/2014/01/140122133713.htm, accessed 28 December 2021

30. Murphy, B, *The Grand Illusion: A synthesis of science and spirituality,*
Book One (Global Freedom Movement Press, 2017), pp 56–57

31. Murphy, B, *The Grand Illusion: A synthesis of science and spirituality,*
Book One (Global Freedom Movement Press, 2017), pp 56–57

32. Epstein, R, 'The empty brain' (Aeon, May 2016), https://aeon.co
/essays/your-brain-does-not-process-information-and-it-is-not
-a-computer, accessed 28 December 2021

33. Davis, N, 'Magic mushrooms show promise in treatment for
depression, study says', *The Guardian* (14 April 2021), www
.theguardian.com/society/2021/apr/14/magic-mushroom
-psilocybin-show-promise-treatment-depression-clinical-trial
-finds, accessed 28 December 2021

34. Hameroff, S, et al, 'Consciousness in the universe: A review of the
'Orch OR' theory' (*Physics of Life Reviews* March 2014), Volume 11,
Issue 1, https://doi.org/10.1016/j.plrev.2013.08.002

35. Fenwick, P, *The Art of Dying* (Continuum, 2008)

36. Moody, R, *Life After Life: The bestselling original investigation that
revealed near-death experiences* (HarperOne, 2015)

37. Alexander, E, *Proof of Heaven: A neurosurgeon's journey into the afterlife* (Piatkus, 2012)

38. Van Lommel, P, *Consciousness Beyond Life: The* Science of the Near-Death Experience (HarperCollins, 2011)

39. Dispenza, J, *Becoming Supernatural: How Common People Are Doing the Uncommon* (Hay House, 2017), p 255

40. Simpson, M, 'A Sister's Eulogy for Steve Jobs', *New York Times* (30 October 2011), www.nytimes.com/2011/10/30/opinion/mona -simpsons-eulogy-for-steve-jobs.html, accessed 28 December 2021

41. Pike, J, 'STAR GATE [Controlled Remote Viewing]' (Federation of American Scientists, December 2005), https://fas.org/irp/program /collect/stargate.htm, accessed 28 December 2021

42. Mastin, L, 'Nonlocality and entanglement' (The Physics of the Universe, no date), www.physicsoftheuniverse.com/topics _quantum_nonlocality.html, accessed 28 December 2021

43. Fernbach, P, 'Why do we believe things that aren't true?' TEDxMileHigh (13 Sept 2017), www.youtube.com/watch?v= jobYTQTgeUE, accessed 2 January 2021

44. Young, E, 'Lifting the lid on the unconscious', *New Scientist* (25 July 2018), www.newscientist.com/article/mg23931880-400-lifting -the-lid-on-the-unconscious, accessed 4 February 2022

45. Doidge, N, *The Brain that Changes Itself: Stories of Personal Triumph from the Frontiers of Brain Science* (Penguin, 2007), pp 46–48

46. de Peyer, R, 'Expert Reveals Why British Schoolchildren Struggle With Maths', *London Evening Standard* (March 2016), www .standard.co.uk/news/education/expert-reveals-why-british -schoolchildren-struggle-with-maths-a3202071.html, accessed 2 January 2021

47. Lipton, B, 'We are programmed to be poor' (1 September 2019), www.youtube.com/watch?v=Qv8k7Et4ss4&list=RDCMUCI _2HqC2a22Q4Jx41o9g72w&start_radio=1&rv=Qv8k7Et4ss4&t=43, accessed 4 February 2022

48. Rothstein, M A, et al. 'The ghost in our genes: Legal and ethical implications of epigenetics', *Health Matrix* (Cleveland, Ohio, 2009) vol. 19,1 pp 1–62, www.ncbi.nlm.nih.gov/pmc/articles/PMC3034450, accessed 4 February 2022

49. Watters, E, 'DNA is not Destiny: The Science of Epigenetics', *Discover* (22 November 2006), www.discovermagazine.com/the -sciences/dna-is-not-destiny-the-new-science-of-epigenetics, accessed 2 January 2021

50. Lipton, B, 'Inner Evolution: Controlling Genetic Expression', Series 1, Episode 6 (Gaia, March 2020), www.gaia.com/video /controlling-genetic-expression, accessed 5 April 2022

51. Lipton, B, *The Biology of Belief: Unleashing the Power of Consciousness, Matter & Miracles* (Hay House, 2011), pp 131–147

52. Henriques, M, 'Can the legacy of trauma be passed down the generations?' (BBC, 26 March 2019), www.bbc.com/future/article/20190326-what-is-epigenetics, accessed 2 January 2022

53. Lipton, B, *The Biology of Belief: Unleashing the Power of Consciousness, Matter & Miracles* (Hay House, 2011), p 44

54. Lipton, B, 'Inner Evolution: Quantum Perceptions of Matter', Series 1, Episode 3 (Gaia, March 2020), www.gaia.com/video/quantum-perceptions-matter, accessed 5 April 2022

55. Max-Planck-Gesellschaft, 'Epigenetics between the generations: We inherit more than just genes' (ScienceDaily, 17 July 2017), www.sciencedaily.com/releases/2017/07/170717100548.htm, accessed 4 February 2022

56. Robson, D, 'Can you think yourself young?', *The Guardian* (2 January 2022), www.theguardian.com/science/2022/jan/02/can-you-think-yourself-young-ageing-psychology

57. Dispenza, J, *Becoming Supernatural: How common people are doing the uncommon* (Hay House, 2017), p xi

58. Callahan, R, Thought Field Therapy (TFT), www.rogercallahan.com/callahan.php

59. Dispenza, J, 'Demystifying Meditation: Rewired with Joe Dispenza, Episode 3' (Gaia, 7 October 2019), www.gaia.com/video/demystifying-meditation, accessed 20 December 2021

60. Neuroscientifically Challenged, 'Know Your Brain: Reticular Formation', Neuroscientifically Challenged (25 July 2015), https://neuroscientificallychallenged.com/posts/know-your-brain-reticular-formation, accessed 4 February 2022

61. Marianne, 'Physics in a minute: The double slit experiment', *Plus Magazine* (19 November 2020), https://plus.maths.org/content/physics-minute-double-slit-experiment-0, accessed 21 December 2021

62. Dispenza, J, *Becoming Supernatural: How common people are doing the uncommon* (Hay House, 2017), pp 206–207

63. Folger, T, 'Does the Universe Exist if We're Not Looking?' *Discover Magazine* (1 June 2002), www.discovermagazine.com/the-sciences/does-the-universe-exist-if-were-not-looking, accessed 3 January 2022

64. Bird, E, 'New way for gut neurons to communicate with the brain', *MedicalNewsToday* (9 August 2020), www.medicalnewstoday.com/articles/new-way-for-gut-neurons-to-communicate-with-the-brain, accessed 21 December 2021

65. Browne, S J, 'What The Vagus Nerve Is And How To Stimulate It For Better Mental Health', *Forbes* (15 April 2021), www.forbes.com/sites/womensmedia/2021/04/15/what-the-vagus-nerve-is-and-how-to-stimulate-it-for-better-mental-health/?sh=e4b45576250c, accessed 4 February 2022

66. Ashami, A M, 'Pain: Is it all in the brain or the heart?'
(*Current Pain and Headache Reports*, November 2014), https://
pubmed.ncbi.nlm.nih.gov/31728781, accessed 21 December 2021

67. HeartMath Institute, 'HeartMath institute science: Scientific
foundation of the heartmath system', www.heartmath.org/science,
accessed 21 December 2021

68. Morales, J, 'The Heart's Electromagnetic Field is Your Superpower',
Psychology Today (29 November 2020), www.psychologytoday
.com/us/blog/building-the-habit-hero/202011/the-hearts
-electromagnetic-field-is-your-superpower, accessed 21 December
2021

69. Brandon, C, 'Visualisation – It's like weight-lifting for the brain',
NPJ (November 2020), https://npjscilearncommunity.nature
.com/posts/visualisation-it-s-like-weight-lifting-for-the-brain,
accessed 21 December 2021

70. HeartMath Institute, 'You Can Change Your DNA', HeartMath
Institute (14 July 2011), www.heartmath.org/articles-of-the-heart
/personal-development/you-can-change-your-dna, accessed 2
January 2022

71. Hancock, R E, 'Super Energies', Work Your Energy podcast (Oct
2019), https://open.spotify.com/episode/3EyZ2FKyPniYXzlET6lzq
L?si=e44c51d778a5464a, accessed 4 February 2022

72. Alderson, J, 'Humans Are Blind to 99.997% of Electromagnetic
Radiation', Medium.com (22 September 2021), https://
medium.com/everyday-science/humans-are-blind-to-99-9-of
-electromagnetic-radiation-f15ec1215109, accessed 4 February 2022

73. Haramein, N, 'Life across the universe: Quantum Revolution,
Episode 9' (Gaia, 31 August 2020), www.gaia.com/video/life
-across-universe and Haramein, N, 'Evidence We Were Never
Alone: Quantum Revolution, Episode 10' (Gaia, 7 September 2020),
www.gaia.com/video/evidence-we-were-never-alone, accessed 16
December 2021

74. Uncommon Descent, 'What great physicists have said about
immateriality and consciousness', Uncommon Descent (11
November 2013), https://uncommondescent.com/physics
/what-great-physicists-have-said-about-immateriality-and
-consciousness, accessed 16 December 2021

75. HubbleSite, 'The Electromagnetic Spectrum' (HubbleSite, last
updated 30 May 2019), https://hubblesite.org/contents/articles
/the-electromagnetic-spectrum, accessed 16 December 2021

76. Haramein, N, 'Life across the universe: Quantum Revolution,
Episode 9' (Gaia, 31 August 2020), www.gaia.com/video/life
-across-universe and N Haramein, 'Evidence We Were Never
Alone: Quantum Revolution, Episode 10' (Gaia, 7 September 2020),
www.gaia.com/video/evidence-we-were-never-alone, accessed 16
December 2021

77. Dispenza, J, *Becoming Supernatural: How common people are doing the uncommon* (Hay House, 2017), p 255

78. Baconnier, S, et al, 'Calcite Microcrystals In The Pineal Gland Of The Human Brain: First physical and chemical studies', (*Bioelectromagnetics*, October 2002), https://pubmed.ncbi.nlm.nih.gov/12224052, accessed 22 December 2021

79. Kaku, M, *Hyperspace: A Scientific Odyssey Through Parallel Universes, Time Warps, and the Tenth Dimension* (OUP, 2016), pp 152–155

80. Trosper, J, 'The universe that we can't see', Futurism (4 April 2015), https://futurism.com/universe-cant-see-infographic, accessed 28 December 2021

81. Pollen, M, 'The Trip Treatment', *The New Yorker* (2 February 2015), www.newyorker.com/magazine/2015/02/09/trip-treatment, accessed 28 December 2021

82. Kaku, M, 'Are There Extra Dimensions?', Closer to Truth (29 January 2016), www.youtube.com/watch?v=RUlVFzl_BJs&t=419s, accessed 28 December 2021

83. Kaku, M, 'The Multiverse has 11 Dimensions', Big Think (31 May 2011), www.youtube.com/watch?v=jI50HN0Kshg, accessed 28 December 2021

84. Jennings, A, 'Telepathy is Real', Inside Science (March 2018), www.youtube.com/watch?v=oZ_M6gYslJE, accessed 28 December 2021

85. Chown, M, 'Our Universe may have a fifth dimension that would change everything we know about physics', Science Focus (4 November 2021), www.sciencefocus.com/space/fifth-dimension, accessed 24 March 2022

86. Bruce, D, The Music of the Solar System (11 March 2021), Savants and Sages, https://savantsandsages.com/2021/03/11/the-music-of-the-solar-system, accessed 4 February 2022

87. Haramein, N, 'Life across the universe: Quantum Revolution, Episode 9' (Gaia, 31 August 2020), www.gaia.com/video/life-across-universe and Haramein, N, 'Evidence We Were Never Alone: Quantum Revolution, Episode 10' (Gaia, 7 September 2020), www.gaia.com/video/evidence-we-were-never-alone, accessed 16 December 2021

88. Guinness World Records, 'Smallest living organism', www.guinnessworldrecords.com/world-records/smallest-living-organism, accessed 28 December 2021

89. McLeod, S, 'Carl Jung', Simply Psychology (21 May 2018), www.simplypsychology.org/carl-jung.html, accessed 6 January 2022

90. India Today web desk, 'Srinivasa Ramanujan: The mathematical genius who credited his 3900 formulae to visions from Goddess Mahalakshmi', *India Today* (26 April 2017), www.indiatoday.in/education-today/gk-current-affairs/story/srinivasa-ramanujan-life-story-973662-2017-04-26, accessed 6 January 2022

91. Kaku, M, *Hyperspace: A scientific odyssey through parallel universes, time warps, and the tenth dimension* (OUP, 2016), p 173

92. Private conversations in May 2020 with Gian Carlo Zazzeri, a shaman and metaphysicist. We discussed the concept of archetypes being physical entities.

93. Hawkins, D R, *Power vs. Force: The hidden determinants of human behaviour* (Hay House, republished 2002) and *Transcending the Levels of Consciousness* (Veritas, 2006)

94. Myss, C, *Archetypes: A beginner's guide to your inner-net* (Hay House, 2013), pp 6–9

95. Von Franz, M L, *Archetypal Dimensions of the Psyche* (Shambhala Publications, 1996), pp 151–152

96. McLeod, S, 'Carl Jung', Simply Psychology (21 May 2018), www.simplypsychology.org/carl-jung.html, accessed 6 January 2022

97. Shamdasani, S, Foreword of *Four Archetypes* by CG Jung, Collected Works of CG Jung, Volume 9, Part 1 (Princeton University Press, 2010)

98. Georgia, A, 'Electrical Activity Inside Humans and Other Animals Is Eerily Similar to Electrical Fields in the Atmosphere', *Newsweek* (5 June 2020), www.newsweek.com/electrical-activity-inside-humans-other-animals-eerily-similar-electrical-fields-atmosphere-1502228, accessed 2 January 2022

99. Gaia TV, 'Chasing the Present' (Gaia, 2019), www.gaia.com/video/chasing-the-present, accessed 4 February 2022

100. Jung, C G, *Alchemical Studies*, Collected Words of C.G. Jung, Volume 13, Paragraph 335 (Princeton University Press 1968)

101. Moskowitz, C, 'Weird! Our universe may be a "multiverse", scientists say', Space.com (12 August 2011), www.space.com/12613-multiverse-universe-eternal-inflation-test.html, accessed 2 January 2022

102. Mind Tasting, 'The Mind of Nikola Tesla and The Power of Visualization', Medium.com (3 Feb 2019), https://mindtasting.medium.com/the-mind-of-nikola-tesla-4305e3d5ee1e, accessed 4 February 2022

103. MacIsaac, T, 'Five Scientific Discoveries Made In Dreams', *The Epoch Times* (4 June 2015), www.theepochtimes.com/5-scientific-discoveries-made-in-dreams_1380669.html, accessed 4 February 2022

104. 'How We Are Conditioned From Childhood For Failure Or Success', Mental Strength (10 July 2021), https://mentalstrength.com/2021/07/10/how-we-are-conditioned-from-childhood-for-failure-or-success, accessed 4 February 2022

105. Hooper, R, 'Hugh Everett: The man who gave us the multiverse theory', *The New Scientist* (September 2014), www.newscientist.com/article/dn26261-hugh-everett-the-man-who-gave-us-the-multiverse, accessed 22 December 2021

106. Tudor, M, et al, 'Hans Berger [1873–1941] – the history of electroencephalography' *Acta medica Croatica*, 2005), https:// pubmed.ncbi.nlm.nih.gov/16334737, accessed 22 December 2021

107. Dispenza, J, 'Changing Your Brainwaves', Rewired, Season 1, Episode 5 (Gaia, 21 October 2019), www.gaia.com/video/changing -your-brainwaves, accessed 4 February 2022

108. Braden, G, 'Brainwave States for Accessing the Divine Matrix, Missing Links', Season 3, Episode 11 (Gaia, 28 March 2019), www .gaia.com/video/brain-states-accessing-divine-matrix, accessed 4 February 2022

109. *Surviving Death: Mediums*, Episode 3 (Netflix, 2021)

110. Harris, RE, et al, 'Neural Correlates of the Shamanic States of Consciousness', *Frontiers in Human Neuroscience* (18 March 2021), https://doi.org/10.3389/fnhum.2021.610466, accessed 2 January 2022

111. Dispenza, J, *Becoming Supernatural: How common people are doing the uncommon* (Hay House, 2017), pp 162–163

112. Gaia staff, 'Rainbow Body 101: Everything you didn't know' (Gaia, 6 March 2020), www.gaia.com/article/rainbow-body-101 -everything-you-didnt-know, accessed 22 December 2021

113. Shmerling, R, 'Right brain/left brain, right?', *Harvard Health Publishing* (November 2019), www.health.harvard.edu/blog/right -brainleft-brain-right-2017082512222, accessed 2 January 2022

114. Dispenza, J, *Becoming Supernatural: How common people are doing the uncommon* (Hay House, 2017), p 193

115. Terrell, S, 'Activate your Hidden 8th Chakra with this secret Technique', Mindvalley (12 September 2018), https://blog .mindvalley.com/8th-chakra, accessed 23 December 2021

116. Krakower, A R, www.jovianarchive.com

117. Professional Wellness Alliance (14 June 2021), https://directory .pwai.us/blog/the-reiki-symbols-explained, accessed 4 February 2022

118. Laszlo, E, *Science and the Akashic Field: An integral theory of everything* (Inner Traditions, Second Edition, 2007), pp 75–78

119. Kaku, M, *Hyperspace: A scientific odyssey through parallel universes, time warps, and the tenth dimension* (OUP, 2016), pp 184–185

120. Nierenberg, C, 'The science of intuition: how to measure hunches and gut feelings', LiveScience (May 2016), www.livescience.com /54825-scientists-measure-intuition.html, accessed 22 December 2021

121. Braden, G, 'Brainwave States for Accessing the Divine Matrix, Missing Links', Season 3, Episode 11 (Gaia, 28 March 2019), www.gaia.com/video/brain-states-accessing-divine-matrix

122. Coelho, P, *The Alchemist* (Thorsons, 1995)

123. Based on conversations with Ingrid Sprake in May 2021. She is a Reiki Master, yoga and meditation trainer, and we discussed her '5 Pillars of Vibration' theory.

124. MacLennan, C, 'What Are Energetic Imprints?', Blissful Light (10 December 2019), www.blissfullight.com/blogs/energy-healing-blog/what-are-energetic-imprints, accessed 4 February 2022

125. The International Centre for Reiki Training: www.reiki.org/faqs/what-history-reiki

126. Kane, L, 'Swift Healing With White Tara: The Rapid Path To Long Life, Merit, Wisdom and Health', Buddha Weekly, https://buddhaweekly.com/swift-healing-white-tara-rapid-path-long-life-merit-wisdom-health, accessed 27 December 2021

127. Seto A, et al, 'Detection of extraordinary large bio-magnetic field strength from the human hand during external Qi emission', Acupuncture & Electro-therapeutics Research, (1992), https://pubmed.ncbi.nlm.nih.gov/1353653, accessed 27 December 2021

128. Peña Ramirez, J., et al. 'The sympathy of two pendulum clocks: beyond Huygens' observations', Scientific Reports 6, Article number 23580 (2016), https://doi.org/10.1038/srep23580, accessed February 4, 2022

129. Round The World Magazine contributor, 'What Are The Solfeggio Frequencies?', Round The World Magazine (8 March 2019), www.roundtheworldmagazine.com/solfeggio-frequencies-2

130. ATUN, 'Bioenergetic Testing – How Does It Work?', ATUN, www.atun.me/about-1, accessed 9 February 2022

131. Meuth, M, 'Bioenergetic Therapy for Advanced Energy Healing', Headway Health, https://headwayhealth.com/headway-health-austin/bioenergetic-therapy-center, accessed 9 February 2022

132. Ewing, D and Chen, L, 'Introduction to Bioenergetic Medicine', Holistic Health Alternatives, https://drdawn.net/learning-center/articles/introduction-to-bioenergetic-medicine, accessed 9 February 2022

133. This information is based on conversations with Andy Hill in June 2021 about bioenergetics and the field of frequency healing.

134. Rose, E, Metaphysical Anatomy: Your body is talking, are you listening? (CreateSpace Independent Publishing Platform, 2012), vol 1, pp 33–35

135. Zeland, V, Reality Transurfing: Steps I–V (CreateSpace Independent Publishing Platform, 2016)

136. Krakower, A R, 'Human design model, Jovian Archive, www.jovianarchive.com/About, accessed 28 December 2021

137. 'Hero's Journey: Definition and Step-by-Step Guide', Reedsy Blog (28 April 2021), https://blog.reedsy.com/guide/story-structure/heros-journey

138. Dispenza, J, Becoming Supernatural: How common people are doing the uncommon (Hay House, 2017), p 85

139. No Author, 'Concept of Collective Unconscious at Jung', Carl Jung Resources, www.carl-jung.net/collective_unconscious.html, accessed 4 February 2022

140. Heyes C, and Catmur C, 'What Happened to Mirror Neurons?', Perspectives on Psychological Science (9 July 2021), 2022;17(1):153–168, https://doi.org/10.1177/1745691621990638, accessed 15 April 2022

141. Hammond, C, 'What We Do and Don't Know About Kindness', BBC (22 September 2021), www.bbc.com/future/article/20210921 -what-we-do-and-dont-know-about-kindness, accessed 4 February 2022

142. Sloman, S, and Fernbach, P, *The Knowledge Illusion: The myth of individual thought and the power of collective wisdom* (Macmillan, 2017)

143. Héctor, G, *Ikigai: The Japanese secret to a long and happy life* (Hutchinson, 2017)

144. Team Human podcast: www.teamhuman.fm

145. Unify: www.facebook.com/unify

146. Resonance Science Foundation: www.resonancescience.org

147. Project Coherence Global Meditation: https://drjoedispenza.com /blogs/dr-joe-s-blog/my-thoughts-on-the-global-meditation?_pos =5&_sid=7243196cb&_ss=r

148. World Peace Group, 'Washington crime study shows 23.3% drop in violent crime trend due to meditating group' (World Peace Group, 2011), www.worldpeacegroup.org/washington_crime _study.html, accessed 29 December 2021

149. World Peace Group, 'Liverpool crime drops 58% in five years' (World Peace Group, 1995), www.worldpeacegroup.org/liverpool _crime_study.html, accessed 29 December 2021

150. Maharishi International University, 'Maharishi Effect', https:// research.miu.edu/maharishi-effect, accessed 4 February 2022

151. Hawkins, D, *Truth Vs. Falsehood: How to tell the difference* (Hay House 2013), pp 97–99

152. Corey, C, 'Superhuman: The Invisible Made Visible', Series 1, Episode 4, Mind Over Matter (Gaia, 2020), www.gaia.com/video /mind-over-matter-0, accessed 2 January 2022

153. Dispenza, J, 'Reality Is Determined by Collective Networks of Observers' (9 October 2021), https://drjoedispenza.com/blogs /dr-joes-blog/reality-is-determined-by-collective-networks-of -observers, accessed 4 February 2022

Acknowledgements

Dr Joe Dispenza, thank you for writing the book that changed my life. There are no words to express my gratitude. Rethink Press, thank you for publishing my book and to your team, who polished it and made it better. Katherine Williams, thank you for the incredible job you did editing this book and grasping what it was I was trying to say. Tori Dee, thank you for the beautiful archetypal images that you drew, they are out of this world. Maria Tansey, thank you for your amazing hypnotherapy and lending me your library of books. Gian Carlo Zazzeri, thank you for our mind-expanding discussions on metaphysics and teaching me how to channel. Ingrid Sprake, thank you for lending me your 'five pillars of vibration' model and introducing me to reiki. Andy Hill, thank you for being a walking encyclopaedia and teaching me about bioenergetic healing. Thank you to all my beta readers: Sirin Ortanca,

Rachel Aitken, Kaja Mohaisen, Ingrid Sprake, Toni Marie Taherian, Solange Van Dijk, Melanie Josey, Lucy Stevenson, Roberta Pagliarini and Hannah Morphey.

Ruth Kudzi, thank you for holding my hand when I needed it most. Jessica Killingley, thank you for expertly guiding me to my first draft and for your laser-sharp insights. Melanie Gow, thank you for your insightful edits and discussion. Eleanor Tweddle, my book buddy, thank you for making me fall off my seat with laughter and our insightful discussions. Samantha Colclough, thank you for your awesome healing hypnotherapy. Natalie Trice, thank you for shining so brightly. Philip Mazloumian, thank you for our insightful conversations. Lynsay Gould, thank you for your wonderful podcasting course – a key part of me learning to 'speak my truth'. Thank you, also, to Sanne Maarschalkerweerd, Kristen Coakley, Melanie Josey, Sirin Ortanca, Solange Van Dijk and Toni Marie Taherian for your ongoing support and to Melanie Tremaine, Laura Weeden and Bhavika Makwana for your business support.

Thank you to my father, Alan Hancock, and stepmother, Margaret Gallagher, who, with their open minds and passion for living and learning, have always inspired me to be the best that I can be and never to give up. My brother, David Hancock, for his deep wisdom and showing me how to walk my own path and to my sister, Caroline Hancock, who has been an inspiration to me all my life and doesn't know how truly talented she is.

And last, but not least, thank you to my husband, Giuseppe Aliberti, and my two beautiful children, who every day inspire me to become a better version of myself while making a positive difference in this beautiful world that we live in.

This book is dedicated to my mother, Roslyn Thorogood, who was born before her time, and as such, lived within the unjust confinements of her society. A truly remarkable and highly intuitive and creative woman, she suffered from crippling self-doubt and low self-esteem all of her life; never fully able to shine in the way that was her human right.

The Author

Ruth Elisabeth Hancock is an author, coach, consultant, speaker and trainer working with entrepreneurs 'energetically' so they can achieve more success, happiness and wealth in their lives.

With a degree in business and a master's in personnel development, Elisabeth has been helping business leaders and owners achieve more success for two decades. However, she realised her field of expertise was too one-dimensional, too focused on external strategies and completely overlooked our inner world of intuition, subtle energy and inner voice.

This inspired her to research the science behind spirituality and study many energy and holistic modalities including energy healing, NLP, shamanic healing, theta healing, reiki, quantum hypnosis, transcendental quantum reiki, meditation and more. Also certified in stress management, clinical nutrition and life coaching, Elisabeth now supports her clients holistically, teaching them how to tap into their true, multidimensional selves and connect with the wisdom in their hearts and soul.

Based in Dubai, Elisabeth has redesigned her family life and business model to accommodate expat living, working from home and home-schooling her children due to her son's learning differences. Her mission is to raise awareness of the unlimited potential of higher consciousness and our energetic universe, which she does through speaking, writing and researching.

To learn more about her transformational journey, you can visit ruthelisabethhancock.com, where you can find out how to work with Elisabeth over Zoom, or access her online learning platform.

Additionally, you can listen to her podcast – Work Your Energy. She discusses all the concepts from this book (and many more…) to help you live better lives by tapping into your energy and the energy around you for more abundance, joy and success.

⊕ ruthelisabethhancock.com
🖸 @workyourenergy
◎ @workyourenergypodcast

Printed in Great Britain
by Amazon